EVERYMAN,
I WILL GO WITH THEE
AND BE THY GUIDE,
IN THY MOST NEED
TO GO BY THY SIDE

EVERYMAN'S LIBRARY
POCKET POETS

BLUES POEMS

*

SELECTED AND
EDITED BY
KEVIN YOUNG

EVERYMAN'S LIBRARY
POCKET POETS

Alfred A. Knopf New York London Toronto

THIS IS A BORZOI BOOK
PUBLISHED BY ALFRED A. KNOPF

This selection by Kevin Young first published in
Everyman's Library, 2003
Copyright © 2003 by Everyman's Library

Sixth printing (US)

A list of acknowledgments to copyright owners appears at the back of
this volume.

All rights reserved. Published in the United States by Alfred A. Knopf,
a division of Random House, Inc., New York, and in Canada by Random
House of Canada Limited, Toronto. Distributed by Random House, Inc.,
New York. Published in the United Kingdom by Everyman's Library,
Northburgh House, 10 Northburgh Street, London EC1V 0AT.
Distributed by Random House (UK) Ltd.

US website: www.randomhouse.com/everymans

ISBN 978-0-375-41458-9 (US)
978-1-84159-758-4 (UK)

A CIP catalogue record for this book is available from the British Library

Typography by Peter B. Willberg

Typeset in the UK by AccComputing, North Barrow, Somerset

Printed and bound in Germany by GGP Media GmbH, Pössneck

CONTENTS

SOME SONGS

9

FOREWORD

There are feelings and states of mind that are hard to describe—some might say that don't properly exist—until we have a word for them. *Catharsis, angst, schadenfreude, duende, ennui*: all feelings we now know in English, but that still retain the tenor of their country and culture of origin. One could easily add *the blues* to this list. Indeed, you might say that the blues contain all these other words in one.

The blues, after all, describe a state of being, a feeling, a form and sound not yet named until their 12 bars and repeated refrains came into being—and now that black folks have invented and named the blues, people all over the world speak them. Being part of our common language in no way denies the blues' origins in African American culture and mouths and hands. Too many people, however, mistake the feeling of the blues with the form of the blues themselves.

For in spite of navigating the depths of despair, the blues ultimately are about triumphing over that despair—or at least surviving it long enough to sing about it. With the blues, the form fights the feeling. Survival and loss, sin and regret, boasts and heartbreak, leaving and loving, a pigfoot and a bottle of beer—the blues are a series of reversals, of finding love and losing it, of wanting to see yourself dead in the depths of despair, and then soon as the train comes down the track, yanking your fool head back. The blues are having the gun, but no bullets to fit it. As one saying goes, the blues ain't nothin' but a good man (or woman) feelin' bad. But another saying knows the opposite is true: the blues ain't nothin' but a bad woman (or man) feelin' good.

Far from a series of sad poems, this collection—the first devoted exclusively to poems about the blues—celebrates life. As Langston Hughes often said, the blues are "laughing to keep from crying"; the fact that this line also appears in the song "Trouble in Mind" tells us that even when there's trouble, we still can laugh about it. We must, the blues insist. Ralph Ellison puts it this way: *The blues is an impulse to keep the painful details and episodes of a brutal experience alive in one's aching consciousness, to finger its jagged grain, and then transcend it, not by the consolation of philosophy but by squeezing from it a near-tragic, near-comic lyricism. As a form, the blues is an autobiographical chronicle of personal catastrophe expressed lyrically.* Indeed, for me the blues provide a fresh way to express the lyric poem's mix of emotion and intensity, all the while evoking not so much strict autobiography as a personal metaphor for life's daily struggles. "You've been a good old wagon, but you done broke down."

The blues can be about work, or the lack of it; about losing hope or your home, your lover or your mind or your faith; or all of these at once! The blues are unafraid of talking about violence, whether of the physical kind (as reflected in Hughes' "Beale Street Love" and Ma Rainey's "See See Rider Blues") or the often more troubling psychological sort. Still, the heartbreak the blues rails against and trains us to overcome is never far from ironic and even comic , and for every "Nobody Knows You When You're Down and Out," Bessie Smith declares "Tain't Nobody's Business if I Do." That Nobody sure is fickle.

The blues ain't polite—they don't say please, though sometimes they say "Good Morning." They are, in the end, often more loyal than that sweet mistreater whom the singer loves but wants "to lay low" with a gun, after feeling low for days. Or nights—the blues after all, began as Saturday night entertainment, making us laugh and move and maybe even forget our troubles, not by pretending everything's all right, but by admitting it's a hard road full of forks and crossroad devils. By finding out that the powerful voice onstage, or on the jukebox, or coming from the radio, has been there too. The blues are loyal to a fault.

What follows gives a sense of the range of poems written in a blues form or in the spirit of the blues, as well as in praise of, or in shared pain with, the blues musicians themselves. The book's first section, "Standards," contains blues poems written before or around World War II, starting with Langston Hughes, the first and greatest poet to write in a blues form. The rest of the section shows the range of poets such as

Leopold Senghor and Muriel Rukeyser, who responded to the blues early on—most recognize not only the personal possibilities of the blues but also the public protest the blues wage against inhumanity by their very insistence on human emotion.

The book's second section, "Some Songs," contains a selection of blues lyrics by the singers and songwriters who popularized and perfected this folk form. You'll find here W. C. Handy, the Father of the Blues and the first to write down the blues as music and lyrics in the nineteen-teens; Mamie Smith, the first to record the blues with "Crazy Blues" (which sold 75,000 copies its first month and started a whole industry of "race records"); Bessie Smith, the Empress of the Blues, whose own "Backwater Blues" charts a historical flood yet speaks volumes about a broader rootlessness; and later and contemporary country blues artists who form a literal lineage from Son House and his brilliant and influential disciple Robert Johnson.

As any listener can tell you, deciphering blues lyrics can often be exactly that, and while in many ways their sliding and slipping of lyrics mirrors the blue notes of the music, the lyrics here are rendered as best as can be. As with translations of poetry, I have scoured for the best, most accurate transcriptions. You'll find the transcribers of lyrics—such as Angela Davis from her *Blues Legacies and Black Feminism* or Eric Sackheim from *The Blues Line*, who help us better to hear—listed below the singers who popularized the songs and (if different) the songwriters.

There are of course many more brilliant blues musicians and lyrics than I could include here: Blind Willie Johnson must stand in for a host of what get called "gospel blues"; Robert Johnson and Bessie Smith could easily command a section each; we end early in the electric blues era with Big Mama Thornton, whose rendition of "Hound Dog" stands as a crucial forerunner of the blues' rebellious baby, rock-n-roll. I have resisted including more recent blues or blues-inspired lyrics largely because these are more widely available. (I have also generally not included artists such as Billie Holiday who arguably stand at the crossroads of blues and jazz—with any luck, such figures may appear in a projected book of jazz poems.) By focusing here on the often hard-to-find classic and country blues, I hope to give those new to the blues and those who admire them already a place to see the songs alongside the poetry inspired by them. When in doubt about whether to include a musician or song, I let the poems decide.

And decide they did. The rest of the book gathers some of the best poems that take the blues as starting point, whether in terms of form, or spirit, or the figures that made the music possible—though often of course a poem evokes a tradition or form without exactly saying so. Indeed the "Form" section sets out not just poets who get at the traditional repetition of the blues, but those like Etheridge Knight who take it as starting point for their own explorations of repetition and feeling; or those, like Sonia Sanchez, who take the clarity of the blues' three lines to invent the blues haiku form. Throughout the book, poets such as Calvin Forbes, Amiri Baraka, and the late June Jordan all evoke what Baraka calls an "envious blues feeling" in search of a blues aesthetic. It seemed for a time that everywhere I looked, the blues were there—from Marilyn Chin's "Blues on Yellow" to Derek Walcott's resigned "Blues" and Joseph Brodsky's plainspoken "Blues" that knows as all blues do, that "Money is green, and I am gray." The poems here are as personal and public, pointed and powerful, as the blues themselves.

Blues Poems provides an introduction and overview that with luck may send you back to your bookshelf or record collection, store or library, or better yet, a live venue in order to hear the blues as poetry, and the poetry of the blues. In reading I hope you'll note the emergence of themes and their submerging and reappearing later, as in a jazz riff—and in this small way even find the many takes on Robert Johnson, or the "Finale" of poems on Bessie Smith, as moving as the music. May the reading of this anthology be full of the discovery and delight I found in editing it, giving a sense of how poets have been enriched by, and enrich, the music that black folks made and the blues name.

KEVIN YOUNG

STANDARDS

Blues Poems before World War II

But if you was to ask me
How de blues they come to be,
Says if you was to ask me
How de blues they come to be—
You wouldn't need to ask me:
Just look at me and see!

LANGSTON HUGHES

THE WEARY BLUES

Droning a drowsy syncopated tune,
Rocking back and forth to a mellow croon,
    I heard a Negro play.
Down on Lenox Avenue the other night
By the pale dull pallor of an old gas light
    He did a lazy sway . . .
    He did a lazy sway . . .
To the tune o' those Weary Blues.
With his ebony hands on each ivory key
He made that poor piano moan with melody.
    O Blues!
Swaying to and fro on his rickety stool
He played that sad raggy tune like a musical fool.
    Sweet Blues!
Coming from a black man's soul.
    O Blues!
In a deep song voice with a melancholy tone
I heard that Negro sing, that old piano moan—
    "Ain't got nobody in all this world,
    Ain't got nobody but ma self.
    I's gwine to quit ma frownin'
    And put ma troubles on the shelf."
Thump, thump, thump, went his foot on the floor.
He played a few chords then he sang some more—

"I got the Weary Blues
And I can't be satisfied.
Got the Weary Blues
And can't be satisfied—
I ain't happy no mo'
And I wish that I had died."
And far into the night he crooned that tune.
The stars went out and so did the moon.
The singer stopped playing and went to bed
While the Weary Blues echoed through his head.
He slept like a rock or a man that's dead.

MORNING AFTER

I was so sick last night I
Didn't hardly know my mind.
So sick last night I
Didn't know my mind.
I drunk some bad licker that
Almost made me blind.

Had a dream last night I
Thought I was in hell.
I drempt last night I
Thought I was in hell.
Woke up and looked around me—
Babe, your mouth was open like a well.

I said, Baby! Baby!
Please don't snore so loud.
Baby! Please!
Please don't snore so loud.
You jest a little bit o' woman but you
Sound like a great big crowd.

BEALE STREET LOVE

Love
Is a brown man's fist
With hard knuckles
Crushing the lips,
Blackening the eyes,—
Hit me again,
Says Clorinda.

SONG FOR A DARK GIRL

Way Down South in Dixie
    (Break the heart of me)
They hung my black young lover
    To a cross roads tree.

Way Down South in Dixie
    (Bruised body high in air)
I asked the white Lord Jesus
    What was the use of prayer.

Way Down South in Dixie
    (Break the heart of me)
Love is a naked shadow
    On a gnarled and naked tree.

MIDWINTER BLUES

In the middle of the winter,
Snow all over the ground.
In the middle of the winter,
Snow all over the ground—
'Twas the night befo' Christmas
My good man turned me down.

Don't know's I'd mind his goin'
But he left me when the coal was low.
Don't know's I'd mind his goin'
But he left when the coal was low.
Now, if a man loves his woman
That ain't no time to go.

He told me that he loved me
But he must a been tellin' a lie.
He told me that he loved me.
He must a been tellin' a lie.
But he's the only man I'll
Love till the day I die.

I'm gonna buy me a rose bud
An' plant it at my back door,
Buy me a rose bud,
Plant it at my back door,
So when I'm dead they won't need
No flowers from the store.

TOO BLUE

I got those sad old weary blues.
I don't know where to turn.
I don't know where to go.
Nobody cares about you
When you sink so low.

What shall I do?
What shall I say?
Shall I take a gun
And put myself away?

I wonder if
One bullet would do?
As hard as my head is,
It would probably take two.

But I ain't got
Neither bullet nor gun—
And I'm too blue
To look for one.

NOTE ON COMMERCIAL THEATRE

You've taken my blues and gone—
You sing 'em on Broadway
And you sing 'em in Hollywood Bowl,
And you mixed 'em up with symphonies
And you fixed 'em
So they don't sound like me.
Yep, you done taken my blues and gone.

You also took my spirituals and gone.
You put me in *Macbeth* and *Carmen Jones*
And all kinds of *Swing Mikados*
And in everything but what's about me—
But someday somebody'll
Stand up and talk about me,
And write about me—
Black and beautiful—
And sing about me,
And put on plays about me!
I reckon it'll be
Me myself!

Yes, it'll be me.

TIRED

I am tired of work; I am tired of building up somebody else's civilization.

Let us take a rest, M'Lissy Jane.

I will go down to the Last Chance Saloon, drink a gallon or two of gin, shoot a game or two of dice and sleep the rest of the night on one of Mike's barrels.

You will let the old shanty go to rot, the white people's clothes turn to dust, and the Calvary Baptist Church sink to the bottomless pit.

You will spend your days forgetting you married me and your nights hunting the warm gin Mike serves the ladies in the rear of the Last Chance Saloon.

Throw the children into the river; civilization has given us too many. It is better to die than it is to grow up and find out that you are colored.

Pluck the stars out of the heavens. The stars mark our destiny. The stars marked my destiny.

I am tired of civilization.

THE HARLEM DANCER

Applauding youths laughed with young prostitutes
And watched her perfect, half-clothed body sway;
Her voice was like the sound of blended flutes
Blown by black players upon a picnic day.
She sang and danced on gracefully and calm,
The light gauze hanging loose about her form;
To me she seemed a proudly-swaying palm
Grown lovelier for passing through a storm.
Upon her swarthy neck black shiny curls
Luxuriant fell; and tossing coins in praise,
The wine-flushed, bold-eyed boys, and even the girls,
Devoured her shape with eager, passionate gaze;
But looking at her falsely-smiling face,
I knew her self was not in that strange place.

MEMORY BLUES

Back again between the odds and ends—
Back again between the odds and ends—
What once was gay's now sad,
What was unknown's now friends.

Each capital's not more than one café
Wherein you lose
yourself in what you have and have had . . .
Why worry choose?

The waiter waits, he'll wait all night—
And when you're tight he'll set you right
Back in tomorrow—or even yesterday . . .
Time plays the piper but what do we pay?

O Bœuf-sur-le-Toit, you had one song—
But when I look in the mirrors it all goes wrong—
Memory Blues—and only back today!
I'm a miserable travelin' man.

COLORED BLUES SINGER

Some weep to find the Golden Pear
Feeds maggots at the core,
And some grow cold as ice, and bear
Them prouder than before.

But you go singing like the sea
Whose lover turns to land;
You make your grief a melody
And take it by the hand.

Such songs the mellow-bosomed maids
Of Africa intone
For lovers dead in hidden glades,
Slow rotting flesh and bone.

Such keenings tremble from the kraal,
Where sullen-browed abides
The second wife whose dark tears fail
To draw him to her sides.

Somewhere Jeritza breaks her heart
On symbols Verdi wrote;
You tear the strings of your soul apart,
Blood dripping note by note.

MA RAINEY

I

When Ma Rainey
Comes to town,
Folks from anyplace
Miles aroun',
From Cape Girardeau,
Poplar Bluff,
Flocks in to hear
Ma do her stuff;
Comes flivverin' in,
Or ridin' mules,
Or packed in trains,
Picknickin' fools . . .
That's what it's like,
Fo' miles on down,
To New Orleans delta
An' Mobile town,
When Ma hits
Anywheres aroun'.

II

Dey comes to hear Ma Rainey from de little river
    settlements,
From blackbottom cornrows and from lumber camps;
Dey stumble in de hall, jes a-laughin' an' a-cacklin',

Cheerin' lak roarin' water, lak wind in river swamps.

An' some jokers keeps deir laughs a-goin' in de
    crowded aisles,
An' some folks sits dere waitin' wid deir aches an'
    miseries,
Till Ma comes out before dem, a-smilin' gold-toofed
    smiles
An' Long Boy ripples minors on de black an' yellow
    keys.

III
O Ma Rainey,
Sing yo' song;
Now you's back
Whah you belong,
Git way inside us,
Keep us strong...

O Ma Rainey,
Li'l an' low;
Sing us 'bout de hard luck
Roun' our do';
Sing us 'bout de lonesome road
We mus' go...

IV

I talked to a fellow, an' the fellow say,
"She jes' catch hold of us, somekindaway.
She sang Backwater Blues one day:

> *'It rained fo' days an' de skies was dark as night,*
> *Trouble taken place in de lowlands at night.*
>
> *'Thundered an' lightened an' the storm begin to roll*
> *Thousan's of people ain't got no place to go.*
>
> *'Den I went an' stood upon some high ol' lonesome hill,*
> *An' looked down on the place where I used to live.'*

An' den de folks, dey natchally bowed dey heads an' cried,
Bowed dey heavy heads, shet dey moufs up tight an' cried,
An' Ma lef' de stage, an' followed some de folks outside."

Dere wasn't much more de fellow say:
She jes' gits hold of us dataway.

CHOICES

Don't want no yaller gal, dat's a color will not stay,
Don't want no yaller, yaller nevah known to stay,
Git caught in a storm, de yaller sho' will fade away.

Don't want no pretty pink, pink ain't de shade fo' me,
Don't want no pretty pink, pink it ain't de shade fo' me.
When you think you's got her, ain't nuffin' but yo' used
    to be.

Don't want no black gal, gums blue lak de sea,
Don't want no blue gums, blue jus' lak de deep blue sea,
Fraid that when I kiss her, bluine run all over me.

Don't want no brownskin, choklit to de bone,
Don't want no brownskin, choklit to de bone,
Choklit melts jes lak vanilla, and runs all out de cone.

Don't want no charcoal, soot's a mess what I despise,
Don't want no charcoal, soot's a mess what I despise,
Want to know whah my gal's at, anytime she shets
    her eyes.

Don't want no Geechie gal, talkin' lak a nachel zoo,
Don't want no Geechie, talkin' lak a nachel zoo,
Jabber lak a monkey, make a monkey outa you.

Don't care for de Ofays, got no dealins wif Miss Ann,
Don't care for de Ofay, got no dealins wif Miss Ann,
Don't lak her brother Hemp, nor her cousin Mr. Cool
Oil Can.

Don't want me no Injin, no Injin squaw of red,
Don't want me no Injin, no Injin squaw of red,
Ain't got much hair, want it left on top my frazzly
head.

Don't want no blue woman, moanin' wid de lonesome
blues,
Don't want no blue woman, moanin' wid de graveyard
blues,
Got mo' blues myself now dan a man could evah use.

Gonna git me a green gal, if a green gal's to be found,
Git me a green gal, if a green gal is to be found,
But I spec' she ain't born yet, and her mama she in the
ground.

HIGH BROWN

Yep, now I gets you, high brown!
High brown, I knows you likes to say
how wide my nose is anyway
like a tie-knot flattened down.

Well, look at yo'self an' see
you ain't no prize to wed.
Yo' mouf is awful big fo' me,
an' yo' naps is short an' red.

So much switchin' wid yo' hips,
jes' so hot!
So much twitchin' wid yo' lips,
jes' so hot!
So much witchin' wid yo' eyes,
jes' so hot!

If you jes' knew de truf,
Miss High Brown,
I loves my coal black gal
and don't need you hangin' 'round.

NICOLÁS GUILLÉN
TRANSLATED BY LANGSTON HUGHES
AND BEN FREDERIC CARRUTHERS

SOOTIE JOE

The years had rubbed out his youth,
But his fellows ranked him still
As a chimney sweep without a peer ...
Whether he raced a weighted corset
Up and down the throat of a freakish flue,
Or, from a chair of rope,
His eyes goggled and his mouth veiled,
He wielded his scraping knife
Through the walled-in darkness.

The soot from ancient chimneys
Had wormed itself into his face and hands.
The four winds had belabored the grime on him.
The sun had trifled with his ebony skin
And left ashen spots.

Sometimes Sootie Joe's wealthy customers
Heard him singing a song that gave them pause:

I's a chimney sweeper, a chimney sweeper,
I's black as the blackest night.
I's a chimney sweeper, a chimney sweeper,
And the world don't treat me right.
But somebody hasta black hisself
For somebody else to stay white.

MELVIN B. TOLSON   37

STREET-LEVEL JAZZ

Eighteen nickels and a rusty, old dime
Slap the scarred mahogany and lead to crime.
Eighteen nickels and a gallon of booze
Bury papa's heart-beats in a soft, black ooze.
Come on, dollar-bill, I'm feeling red—
Jump and stagger till I find a swampy bed.
Slip in, Blues, I'm going to make you loud
Till I spread my sugar on a dark, brown shroud.
Listen, babe, I've got to fly south-east,
Nothing on and happy on a cake of yeast!
Pay me, friend, I'm spreading five out black.
Kiss your mean-eyed pain and buy another stack.
Fret my bones!—you're bluffing on ace-high?
Take your old bandanna out and start to cry.
Twist my lip!—she stole your diamond-pin?
Charge it up to laughy-gin and stay right in!
Rip my thigh!—you took a double-cross?
Say it with banana-spiels and trip that boss!
Look out, girl, I've sold my last bouquet—
Keep your eyes on papa's face or start to pray.
Go 'way, love, you're like a forty-four.
Riddled now with bullet-holes—I can't take more.
Aw, now, love, I never meant that line.
Every man's a hairy baby when you shine.
Hug me, night, you've got a bughouse sigh.

Morning scrapes me cold, but you're a velvet lie.
Slug me, night, and give me big-boy dreams—
Stepping on the air and full of lowdown schemes.
What is life except a chance to bluff,
Hiding all the dirty sores where days got rough?
Take it fast and twirl a nasty lip.
All you get is toe and boot-heel when you slip . . .
I've got the dark, stark, long-nailed blues:
I've got an old, black screamy mood.
My heart's a room with nasty news
Enough to make an angel brood.
I'll take a long, deep, raspy breath
And walk right down those railroad-ties.
But when I keep my date with death
He'll find a straight look in my eyes!

BLUES
For Hedli Anderson

Ladies and gentlemen, sitting here,
Eating and drinking and warming a chair,
Feeling and thinking and drawing your breath,
Who's sitting next to you? It may be Death.

As a high-stepping blondie with eyes of blue
In the subway, on beaches, Death looks at you;
And married or single or young or old,
You'll become a sugar daddy and do as you're told.

Death is a G-man. You may think yourself smart,
But he'll send you to the hot-seat or plug you through
    the heart;
He may be a slow worker, but in the end
He'll get you for the crime of being born, my friend.

Death as a doctor has first-class degrees;
The world is on his panel; he charges no fees;
He listens to your chest, says—"You're breathing.
    That's bad.
But don't worry; we'll soon see to that, my lad."

Death knocks at your door selling real estate,
The value of which will not depreciate;

40

It's easy, it's convenient, it's old world. You'll sign,
Whatever your income, on the dotted line.

Death as a teacher is simply grand;
The dumbest pupil can understand.
He has only one subject and that is the Tomb;
But no one ever yawns or asks to leave the room.

So whether you're standing broke in the rain,
Or playing poker or drinking champagne,
Death's looking for you, he's already on the way,
So look out for him to-morrow or perhaps to-day.

W. H. AUDEN   41

FUNERAL BLUES

Stop all the clocks, cut off the telephone,
Prevent the dog from barking with a juicy bone,
Silence the pianos and with muffled drum
Bring out the coffin, let the mourners come.

Let aeroplanes circle moaning overhead
Scribbling on the sky the message He Is Dead,
Put crêpe bows round the white necks of the public
    doves,
Let the traffic policemen wear black cotton gloves.

He was my North, my South, my East and West,
My working week and my Sunday rest,
My noon, my midnight, my talk, my song;
I thought that love would last for ever: I was wrong.

The stars are not wanted now; put out every one,
Pack up the moon and dismantle the sun,
Pour away the ocean and sweep up the wood;
For nothing now can ever come to any good.

GEORGE ROBINSON: BLUES

Gauley Bridge is a good town for Negroes, they let us
      stand around, they let us stand
around on the sidewalks if we're black or brown.
Vanetta's over the trestle, and that's our town.

The hill makes breathing slow, slow breathing after
      you row the river,
and the graveyard's on the hill, cold in the springtime
      blow,
the graveyard's up on high, and the town is down
      below.

Did you ever bury thirty-five men in a place in back of
      your house,
thirty-five tunnel workers the doctors didn't attend,
died in the tunnel camps, under rocks, everywhere,
      world without end.

When a man said I feel poorly, for any reason, any
      weakness or such,
letting up when he couldn't keep going barely,
the Cap and company come and run him off the job
      surely.

I've put them
DOWN from the tunnel camps
to the graveyard on the hill,
tin-cans all about—it fixed them!—

TUNNELITIS
hold themselves up
at the side of a tree,
I can go right now
to that cemetery.

When the blast went off the boss would call out, Come,
        let's go back,
when that heavy loaded blast went white, Come, let's
        go back,
telling us hurry, hurry, into the falling rocks and muck.

The water they would bring had dust in it, our
        drinking water,
the camps and their groves were colored with the dust,
we cleaned our clothes in the groves, but we always
        had the dust.
Looked like somebody sprinkled flour all over the
        parks and groves,
it stayed and the rain couldn't wash it away and it
        twinkled
that white dust really looked pretty down around our
        ankles.

As dark as I am, when I came out at morning after the
    tunnel at night,
with a white man, nobody could have told which man
    was white.
The dust had covered us both, and the dust was white.

NDÉSSÉ, OR *"BLUES"*

Spring rained its icy water on all my unleashed desires,
My young sap gushed with the first touch of tender bark.
Now in the heart of July, I am blinder than Winter is at
the pole.
My wings beat and break against the bars of the low sky
No ray of sun can pierce the soundless vault of my ennui.
What sign to recover? What keys to strike?
How can I reach the god of long-distance spears?
The royal summer of the South, down there, would arrive
Too late, yes, and in agonizing September!
In which book can I find the fervor of your reverberation?
In the pages of which book, on whose unreachable lips,
Find your delirious love?
My restless waiting wears me out. Oh, the sound of rain
On the monotonous leaves!
Just play me "Solitude," Duke, so I can cry myself to sleep.

GUITAR

Ma six string guitar with the lonesome sound
Can't hold its own against a Georgia hound.

O mamma when the sun goes the downstairs way
And the night spreads out an the moon make day,

I sits with ma feet raised to the rail
And sings the song bout ma buddy in jail:

> *In the red-dirt land,*
> *And the pine tree high,*
> *Gonna find me peace*
> *By-an-by.*
>
> *Gonna find me a baby*
> *Some pretty-eye gal*
> *To be ma mother*
> *Ma wife an pal.*
>
> *Ain't had nobody*
> *To call me home*
> *From the electric cities*
> *Where I roam.*

Yes, I been travelin
Over all
To find a place
What I could call
Home, baby,
Sweet cotton-field home . . .

When I gets to the place where a cracker got mad,
Struck ma fine buddy, struck all I had,
The hound start howlin till the stars break down
An make ma song like a boat what's drown.

Ma six string guitar with the lonesome sound
Can't hold its own against that Georgia hound.

BLUES STANZAS

Lord, Lord, how night falls
South of the Mason-Dixon, presses down,
And one bird in the lonely light calls—
Lord, others answer, answer all around.

John Henry struck, I heard his hammer ringing,
Said, every man, said, every man today
Over that mountain heard John Henry singing,
And there were green hills, green hills far away.

RED CLAY BLUES

I miss that red clay, Lawd, I
Need to feel it on my shoes.
Says miss that red clay, Lawd, I
Need to feel it on my shoes.
I want to see Georgia, cause I
Got them red clay blues.

Pavement's hard on my feet. I'm
Tired o'this concrete street.
Pavement's hard on my feet, I'm
Tired o'this city street.
Goin' back to Georgia where
That red clay can't be beat.

I want to tramp in the red mud, Lawd, and
Feel the red clay round my toes.
I want to wade in the red mud,
Feel that red clay suckin' at my toes.
I want my little farm back and I
Don't care where that landlord goes.

I want to be in Georgia, when the
Big storms start to blow.
Yes I want to be in Georgia when that
Big storm starts to blow.

I want to see the landlords runnin' cause I
Wonder where they gonna go!

I got them red clay blues.

THE FB EYE BLUES

That old FB eye
Tied a bell to my bed stall
Said old FB eye
Tied a bell to my bed stall
Each time I love my baby, gover'ment knows it all.

Woke up this morning
FB eye under my bed
Said I woke up this morning
FB eye under my bed
Told me all I dreamed last night, every word I said.

Everywhere I look, Lord
I see FB eyes
Said everywhere I look, Lord
I find FB eyes
I'm getting sick and tired of gover'ment spies.

My mama told me
A rotten egg'll never fry
Said my mama told me
A rotten egg'll never fry
And everybody knows a cheating dog'll never thrive.

Got them blues, blues, blues
Them mean old FB eye blues
Said I got them blues, blues, blues
Them dirty FB eye blues
Somebody tell me something, some good news.

DICTY BLUES

I regret to inform you that the lady has gone away
I am sorry to inform you that the lady has gone away
The lady was in arrears. She couldn't stay. She jest
    took out

Said I find myself embarrassed by pecuniary distress
    Yes
It grieves me to confess my acute financial distress
The condition of my fortune is unfortunately more
    or less

Will the prepossessing lady in the black net ruffles *Uh*
The captivating lady in the black net ruffles *Uh*
Consent to join me in a dish of hare and truffles? *Uh*

What you tawkin about, man?

DOWN-HOME BOY

I'm a down-home boy
trying to get ahead.
It seems like I go
backwards instead.

Been in Chicago
over a year.
Had nothing down home,
not much here.

A measly job,
a greedy boss—
that's how come
I left Waycross.

Those Great Lake winds
blow all around:
I'm a light-coat man
in a heavy-coat town.

CARRY ME BACK

Carry me back to old Virginia.
    Magnolia blossoms fill the air.
Carry me back to old Virginia:
    the only way you'll get me there.

LET ME TELL YOU BLUES SINGERS
SOMETHING

Let me tell you blues singers something,
one thing maybe that you do not know.
Let me tell you blues singers something,
one thing maybe that you do not know.
The songs of the Lord will take you down any
kind of lonely old road you may have to go.

QUEEN OF THE BLUES

Mame was singing
At the Midnight Club.
And the place was red
With blues.
She could shake her body
Across the floor.
For what did she have
To lose?

She put her mama
Under the ground
Two years ago.
(Was it three?)
She covered that grave
With roses and tears.
(A handsome thing
To see.)

She didn't have any
Legal pa
To glare at her,
To shame
Her off the floor
Of the Midnight Club.
Poor Mame.

She didn't have any
Big brother
To shout
"No sister of mine! . . ."
She didn't have any
Small brother
To think she was everything
Fine.

She didn't have any
Baby girl
With velvet
Pop–open eyes.
She didn't have any
Sonny boy
To tell sweet
Sonny boy lies.

"Show me a man
What will love me
Till I die.
Now show me a man
What will love me
Till I die.
Can't find no such a man
No matter how hard
You try.

Go 'long, baby.
Ain't a true man left
In Chi.

"I loved my daddy.
But what did my daddy
Do?
I loved my daddy.
But what did my daddy
Do?
Found him a brown-skin chicken
What's gonna be
Black and blue.

"I was good to my daddy.
Gave him all my dough.
I say, I was good to my daddy.
I gave him all of my dough.
Scrubbed hard in them white folks'
Kitchens
Till my knees was rusty
And so'."

The M.C. hollered,
"Queen of the blues!
Folks, this is strictly
The queen of the blues!"

She snapped her fingers.
She rolled her hips.
What did she have
To lose?

But a thought ran through her
Like a fire.
"Men don't tip their
Hats to me.
They pinch my arms
And they slap my thighs.
But when has a man
Tipped his hat to me?"

Queen of the blues!
Queen of the blues!
Strictly, strictly,
The queen of the blues!

Men are low down
Dirty and mean.
Why don't they tip
Their hats to a queen?

SOME SONGS

And if someone asks you
who sang this song
Tell 'em old black boy's
been here and gone

TRADITIONAL

ST. LOUIS BLUES

I hate to see de ev'nin' sun go down,
Hate to see de ev'nin' sun go down,
'Cause ma baby, he done lef dis town.

Feelin' tomorrow lak ah feel today,
Feel tomorrow lak ah feel today,
I'll pack my trunk, make ma gitaway.

St. Louis woman, wid her diamon' rings,
Pulls dat man roun' by her apron strings.
'Twant for powder an' for store-bought hair,
De man ah love would not gone nowhere, nowhere.

Got de St. Louis Blues jes as blue as ah can be,
Dat man got a heart lak a rock cast in the sea,
Or else he wouldn't have gone so far from me.

Been to de Gypsy to get ma fortune tole,
To de Gypsy done got ma fortune tole,
'Cause I'm most wile 'bout ma Jelly Roll.

Gypsy done tole me, "Don't you wear no black."
Yes she done tole me, "Don't you wear no black,
Go to St. Louis. You can win him back."

Help me to Cairo, make St. Louis by maself,
Git to Cairo, find ma ole friend Jeff.
Gwine to pin maself close to his side,
If ah flag his train, I sho' can ride.

I loves dat man lak a schoolboy loves his pie,
Lak a Kentucky Col'nel loves his mint an' rye,
I'll love ma baby till the day ah die.

You ought to see dat stovepipe brown of mine,
Lak he owns de Dimon Joseph line,
He'd make a cross-eyed 'oman go stone blin'.

Blacker than midnight, teeth lak flags of truce,
Blackest man in de whole St. Louis,
Blacker de berry, sweeter am de juice.

About a crap game, he knows a pow'ful lot,
But when work-time comes, he's on de dot.
Gwine to ask him for a cold ten-spot,
What it takes to git it, he's cert'nly got.

A black-headed gal makes a freight train jump the
          track,
Said a black-headed gal makes a freight train jump
          the track,
But a long tall gal makes a preacher ball the Jack.

Lawd, a blonde-headed woman makes a good man leave
    the town,
I said blonde-headed woman makes a good man leave
    the town,
But a red-headed woman makes a boy slap his papa
    down.

Oh ashes to ashes and dust to dust,
I said ashes to ashes and dust to dust,
If my blues don't get you my jazzing must.

W. C. HANDY   65

CRAZY BLUES

I can't sleep at night
I can't eat a bite
'Cause the man I love
He don't treat me right

He makes me feel so blue
I don't know what to do
Sometimes I'm sad inside
And then begin to cry
'Cause my best friend . . . said his last goodbye

There's a change in the ocean
Change in the deep blue sea . . . my baby
I tell you folks there . . . ain't no change in me
My love for that man
Will always be

Now I've got the crazy blues
Since my baby went away
I ain't got no time to lose
I must find him today
Now the doctor's gonna do all . . . that he can
But what you gonna need is a undertaker man
I ain't had nothin' but bad news
Now I've got the crazy blues

Now I can read his letter
I sure can't read his mind
I thought he's lovin' me ...
He's leavin' all the time
Now I see ...
My poor love was lyin'

I went to the railroad
Hang my head on the track
Thought about my daddy
I gladly snatched it back
Now my babe's gone
And gave me the sack

Now I've got the crazy blues
Since my baby went away
I ain't had no time to lose
I must find him today
I'm gonna do like a Chinaman ... go and get some hop
Get myself a gun ... and shoot myself a cop
I ain't had nothin' but bad news
Now I've got the crazy blues

Those blues

MAMIE SMITH, COMPOSED BY PERRY BRADFORD   67
TRANSCRIBED BY ADAM GUSSON

SEE SEE RIDER BLUES

I'm so unhappy, I feel so blue
I always feel so sad

I made a mistake, right from the start
Lord, it seems so hard to part

Oh, but this letter that I will write
I hope he will remember, when he receives it

See, see, rider, see what you done done, Lord, Lord,
    Lord
Made me love you, now your gal done come
You made me love you, now your gal done come

I'm going away, baby, won't be back 'til fall, Lord,
    Lord, Lord
Goin' away, baby, won't be back 'til fall
If I find me a good man, I won't be back at all

I'm gonna buy me a pistol, just as long as I am tall,
    Lord, Lord, Lord
Gonna kill my man and catch the Cannonball
If he don't have me, he won't have no gal at all.

     TRANSCRIBED BY ANGELA DAVIS

EMPTY BED BLUES

I woke up this mornin' with an awful achin' head
I woke up this mornin' with a awful achin' head
My new man had left me just a room and a empty bed

Bought me a coffee grinder, got the best one I could
    find
Bought me a coffee grinder, got the best one I could
    find
So he could grind my coffee, 'cause he had a brand
    new grind

He's a deep sea diver with a stroke that can't go wrong
He's a deep sea diver with a stroke that can't go wrong
He can touch the bottom and his wind holds out so
    long

He knows how to thrill me and he thrills me night
    and day
Lord, he knows how to thrill me, he thrills me night
    and day
He's got a new way of lovin' almost takes my breath
    away

Lord, he's got that sweet somethin', and I told my gal
    friend Lou
He's got that sweet somethin', and I told my gal friend
    Lou
From the way she's ravin', she must have gone and
    tried it too.

When my bed get empty, make me feel awful mean
    and blue
When my bed get empty, make me feel awful mean
    and blue
My springs are gettin' rusty', sleepin' single like I do

Bought him a blanket, pillow for his head at night
Bought him a blanket, pillow for his head at night
Then I bought him a mattress so he could lay just right

He came home one evening with his spirit way up high
He came home one evening with his spirit way up high
What he had to give me made me wring my hands
    and cry

He give me a lesson that I never had before
He give me a lesson that I never had before
When he got through teachin' me, from my elbow
    down was sore

He boiled my first cabbage and he made it awful hot
He boiled my first cabbage and he made it awful hot
Then he put in the bacon, it overflowed the pot

When you get good lovin', never go and spread the
news
Yeah, it will double cross you and leave you with them
empty bed blues.

BESSIE SMITH
COMPOSED BY J. C. JOHNSON

BACKWATER BLUES

When it rains five days and the skies turn dark as night
When it rains five days and the skies turn dark as night
Then trouble's takin' place in the lowlands at night

I woke up this mornin', can't even get out of my door
I woke up this mornin', can't even get out of my door
That's enough trouble to make a poor girl wonder where
she wanna go

Then they rowed a little boat about five miles 'cross
the pond
Then they rowed a little boat about five miles 'cross
the pond
I packed all my clothes, throwed 'em in and they rowed
me along

When it thunders and lightnin', and the wind begins
to blow
When it thunders and lightnin', and the wind begins
to blow
There's thousands of people ain't got no place to go

Then I went and stood upon some high old lonesome hill
Then I went and stood upon some high old lonesome hill
Then looked down on the house where I used to live

Backwater blues done caused me to pack my things and go
Backwater blues done caused me to pack my things and go
'Cause my house fell down and I can't live there no mo'

Mmmmmmmmmm, I can't move no mo'
Mmmmmmmmmm, I can't move no mo'
There ain't no place for a poor old girl to go.

GIMME A PIGFOOT

[SPOKEN]
Twenty-five cents? Hah! No, no, I wouldn't pay twenty-
    five cents to go in nowhere, 'cause listen here ...

[SUNG]
Up in Harlem every Saturday night
When the highbrows get together it's just too tight

They all congregates at an all night strut
And what they do is tut, tut, tut

Ole Hannah Brown from 'cross town
Gets full of corn and starts breakin' 'em down

Just at the break of day
You can hear old Hannah say

Gimme a pigfoot and a bottle of beer
Send me, gate, I don't care

I feel just like I wanna clown
Give the piano player a drink because he's bringin'
    me down

He's got rhythm, yeah, when he stomps his feet
He sends me right off to sleep

Check all your razors and your guns
We gonna be rasslin' when the wagon comes

I want a pigfoot and a bottle of beer
Send me, 'cause I don't care
Slay me, 'cause I don't care

Gimme a pigfoot and a bottle of beer
Send me, gate, I don't care

I feel just like I wanna clown
Give the piano player a drink because he's bringin'
        me down

He's got rhythm, yeah, when he stomps his feet
He sends me right off to sleep

Check all your razors and your guns
Do the shim sham shimmy 'til the risin' sun

Gimme a reefer and a gang o' gin
Slay me, 'cause I'm in my sin
Slay me, 'cause I'm full of gin.

BESSIE SMITH, COMPOSED BY LEOLA B. WILSON   75
AND WESLEY "SOCKS" WILSON
TRANSCRIBED BY ANGELA DAVIS

WILD WOMEN DON'T HAVE THE BLUES

I've got a disposition and a way of my own,
When my man starts to kicking I let him find a
    new home,
I get full of good liquor, walk the street all night,
Go home and put my man out if he don't act right.
Wild women don't worry,
Wild women don't have the blues.

You never get nothing by being an angel child,
You'd better change your ways an' get real wild.
I wanta' tell you something, I wouldn't tell you no lie,
Wild women are the only kind that ever get by.
Wild women don't worry,
Wild women don't have the blues.

TROUBLE IN MIND

Trouble in mind, I'm blue,
But I won't be blue always,
For the sun will shine in my backdoor someday.

Trouble in mind, that's true,
I have almost lost my mind;
Life ain't worth livin', feel like I could die,

I'm gonna lay my head on some lonesome railroad line:
Let the two nineteen train ease my troubled mind.

Trouble in mind, I'm blue,
My poor heart is beatin' slow;
Never had no trouble in my life before.

I'm all alone at midnight,
And my lamp is burning low,
Never had so much trouble in my life before.

I'm gonna lay my head
On that lonesome railroad track,
But when I hear the whistle,
Lord, I'm gonna pull it back.

I'm goin' down to the river
Take along my rocking chair,
And if the blues don't leave me,
I'll rock on away from there.

Well, trouble, oh, trouble,
Trouble on my worried mind,
When you see me laughin',
I'm laughin' just to keep from cryin'.

78   RICHARD M. JONES

JESUS MAKE UP MY DYING BED

Since me and Jesus got: married
Haven't been a minute apart
With the receiver in my hand
And re-ligion in my heart

I can ring 'im up easy
Ahhhhhhhhh
Oh well
Ring 'im up easy
Go make up my

Mmmm
Weeping   that he ain't: lost
They despied the Amen
Hanging on the Cross

Hanging there in misery
Ahhhhhhhhh
Oh well
Hanging there in misery
Go make up my

Mmmmmmmmmmmmmmmm
Mmmmmm mmmmmmmmmm
Jesus gon' make up my

They despied the: Amen
Made poor Martha moan
Jesus said to his de-sciples
Come and carry my mother along

Dying will be easy
Ahhhhhhhhh
Dying will be easy
Dying will be easy
Jesus gon' make up my

I'm dead and: buried
Some body said that I was lost
When it get down to Jordan
Have to bear my *body* across

Done gone over
Ahhhhhhhhh
Oh well
Done gone over
Make up my

DEATH LETTER BLUES

I got a letter this morning
How do
You reckon it read?

It said Honey, the gal
You love is dead

I got a letter this morning
Mmmm, How do you reckon it read?

You know it said Hurry, Hurry
'Cause the gal you love is dead

*

Oh I grabbed up my suitcase
Took out down the road
When I got there she was laying
On the cooling board

I grabbed up my suitcase
And I say I took off down the road
I say but when I got there
She was laying on the cooling board

*

Well I walked up right close
Looked down in her face

Said Good old girl
Gotta lay there till Judgement Day

I walked up right close
I say and I looked down in her face

I said The good old girl
Gotta lay there till Judgement Day

*

Look like it was ten thousand people
Standing round the burying ground
I didn't know I loved her
Till they let her down

Look like ten thousand
Were standing round the burying ground

You know I didn't know that I loved her
Till they began to let her down

*

Well I folded up my arms
I slow walked away

I said Farewell Honey
I'll see you Judgement Day

Yeah, Oh yes,
I walked away

I said Farewell Farewell
I'll see you Judgement Day

*

You know I didn't feel so bad
Till the good old sun went down:
I didn't have a soul
To throw my arms around

I didn't feel so bad
Until the good old sun went down

Mmmmm Hm Mmmm

*

You know it's so hard to love
Someone who don't love you
Ain't satisfaction
Don't care what you do

Yeah it's so hard
To love someone don't love you

You know it look like it ain't satisfaction
Don't care what you do

*

Well I got up this morning
Break of day
Just hugging the pillow
She used to lay

I said, shoooo, this morning
Yes, at the break of day

You know I hugged the pillow
where my good gal used to lay

*

When I got up this morning
feeling bad from my shoes

You know I
musta had the walking blues

Shoooo this morning
a feeling from my shoes

Oh I
musta had the walking blues

*

Oh hush—

Thought I heard her call my name

It wasn't so loud
So nice and clean

Yeah

Mmm Mmm Hmm Mmm

Hmmm Hmmm Hmm

KINDHEARTED WOMAN BLUES
Take 2

I got a kindhearted mama
Do anything in this world for me

I got a kindhearted mama
Do anything in this world for me

But these evil-hearted women
Man they will not let me be

I love my baby
But my baby don't love me

I love my baby wooo
My baby don't love me

I really love that woman
Can't stand to leave her be

It ain't but one thing
Makes Mister Johnson drink

I get low bout how you treats me baby
I begin to think

Oh babe
Our love don't feel the same

You break my heart
When you call Mister So & So's name

She's a kindhearted mama
She studies evil all the time

She's a kindhearted woman
She studies evil all the time

You best to kill me baby
Just to have it on my mind

Someday someday
I will shake your hand goodbye

Someday someday
I will shake your hand goodbye

I can't give any more of my lovin'
Cause I just ain't satisfied

ROBERT JOHNSON

87

TRANSCRIBED BY KEVIN YOUNG

HELLHOUND ON MY TRAIL

I've got to keep moving
  I've got to keep moving
           blues falling down like hail
           blues falling down like hail
Ummmmmmmmmmmmmmmmmmmmmm
           blues falling down like hail
           blues falling down like hail
And the days keeps on 'minding me
        there's a hellhound on my trail
        hellhound on my trail
          hellhound on my trail

If today was Christmas Eve
  If today was Christmas Eve
        and tomorrow was Christmas
        Day
If today was Christmas Eve
        and tomorrow was Christmas
        Day
        (aw wouldn't we have a
        time baby)
All I would need my little sweet rider just
        to pass the time away
        uh huh
        to pass the time away

You sprinkled hot foot powder
                    umm around my door
                    all around my door
You sprinkled hot foot powder
                    all around your daddy's door
                    hmmm hmmm hmmm
It keeps me with a rambling mind, rider,
                    every old place I go
                    every old place I go

I can tell the wind is rising
                    the leaves trembling on
                    the trees
                    trembling on the trees
I can tell the wind is rising
                    leaves trembling on the trees
                    umm hmm hmm hmm
All I need my little sweet woman
                    and to keep my company
                    hmmm hmmm hmmm
                    hmmm
                    my company

ROBERT JOHNSON   89
TRANSCRIBED BY ERIC SACKHEIM

LOVE IN VAIN
Take 1

I followed her
    to the station
        with a suitcase in my hand

And I followed her to the station
    a suitcase in my hand

Well it's hard to tell
    it's hard to tell
        when all your love's in vain

All my love's in vain

When the train
    pulled up to the station
        I looked her in the eye

When the train rolled up to the station
    And I looked her in the eye

Well I was lonesome
    I felt so lonesome
        that I could not help but cry

All my love's in vain

The train
    it left the station
        with two lights on behind

When the train
    it left the station
        two lights on behind

Well
    The blue light was my blues
        And the red light was my mind

All my love's in vain

Eeeee
    Whooo wheeley may
        Wooo oh woe

All my love's in vain

ROBERT JOHNSON   91
TRANSCRIBED BY KEVIN YOUNG

SENT FOR YOU YESTERDAY

Don't the moon look lonesome shining through the
    trees?
Don't the moon look lonesome shining through the
    trees?
Don't your house look lonesome when your baby's
    packed up to leave?

Yeah, she's little and low and built up from the ground,
She's little and low and built up from the ground.
Just a while before day she'll make your love come
    down.

Sent for you yesterday, and here you come today,
Sent for you yesterday, and here you come today
Baby, you can't love me and treat me thataway.

GOOD MORNING BLUES

[SPOKEN]
Now this is the blues. Never was a white man had the
blues, 'cause nothin' to worry about.   Now you lay
down at night, you roll from one side of the bed to the
other all night long.   You can't sleep.   What's the
matter?   The blues has got you.   You get up and sit on
the side of your bed in the mornin'.   May have a sister
and a brother, mother and father around, but you don't
want no talk out of 'em.   What's the matter?   The
blues got you.   Well, you go and put your feet under
the table, look down in your plate, got everything you
want to eat.   But you shake your head and you get up
and say, "Lord, I can't eat and I can't sleep."   What's
the matter?   The blues got you.   Wanna talk to you.
Here what you got to tell 'em.

[SUNG]
Good mornin', blues, blues how do you do?
Good mornin', blues, blues how do you do?
I'm doin' all right, good mornin', how are you?

I lay down last night, turnin' from side to side.
Oh, turnin' from side to side.
I was not sick but I was just dissatisfied.

When I got up this mornin' with the blues walkin'
    'round my bed.
Oh, with the blues walkin' 'round my bed.
I went to eat my breakfast, blues was all in my bread.

Good mornin', blues, blues how do you do?
Oh, blues how do you do?
I'm doin' all right, good mornin', how are you?

Lord, a brownskin woman'll make a moon-eyed man
    go blind.
Oh, she will make a moon-eyed man go blind.
And a jet black woman'll make you take your time.

Good mornin', blues, blues how do you do?
Oh, blues how do you do?
I'm doin' all right, good mornin', how are you?

TRANSCRIBED BY R R MACLEOD

HOOCHIE COOCHIE MAN

The Gypsy woman told my mother
Before I was born
I got a boy child's coming
He gonna be a son of a gun

He gonna make pretty womens
Jump and shout
Then the world wanna know
What this all about

But you know I'm here
Everybody knows I'm here
Well you know I'm the hoochie coochie man
Everybody knows I'm here

I got a black cat bone
I got a mojo too
I got the John the Conqueror root
I'm gonna mess with you

I'm gonna make you girls
Lead me by my hand
Then the world'll know
The hoochie coochie man

But you know I'm here
Everybody knows I'm here
Well you know I'm the hoochie coochie man
Everybody knows I'm here

On the seventh hour
On the seventh day
On the seventh month
The seventh doctor say:
He was born for good luck
And that you'll see
I got seven hundred dollars
Don't you mess with me

You know I'm here
Everybody knows I'm here
Well you know I'm the hoochie coochie man
Everybody knows I'm here

MUDDY WATERS
COMPOSED BY WILLIE DIXON

HOUND DOG

You ain't
Nothing but a hound dog
Just snooping round my door

Ain't nothing but a hound dog
That's snooping round my door

You can wag your tail
But I ain't gonna feed you no more

You told me you were high class
I can see through that

Told me you were high class
But I can see through that

Daddy I know
You ain't no real cool cat

You ain't nothing but a hound dog
Snooping round the door

Just an old hound dog
That's snooping round my door

You can wag your tail
But I ain't gonna feed you
No more

(Oh yeah)
(Make it feel so good)

Make me feel so blue
Make me weep and moan

Make me feel so blue
Honey you make me weep and moan

Ain't looking for a woman
All you looking is for home

Ain't nothing but a hound dog
been snooping round the door

Just an old hound dog
been snooping round my door

You can wag your tail
But I ain't going to feed
you no more

(And bow-wow to you too honey!)

98   BIG MAMA THORNTON, COMPOSED BY
     JERRY LEIBER AND MIKE STOLLER
     TRANSCRIBED BY KEVIN YOUNG

FORM

You know the blues ain't nothing but a
          Low down shaking
          Low down shaking
          Aching chill
I say the blue-ues
          Is a low down
          Old aching chill
Well if you ain't had 'em honey,
          I hope you ne-
          Ver will

SON HOUSE
The Jinx Blues
BY BIG JOE WILLIAMS

YOU KNOW
(For the people who speak the you know language)

You know
   i sure would like to write a blues
you know
   a nice long blues
you know
   a good feeling piece to my writing hand
you know
   my hand that can bring two pieces of life
   together in your ear
you know
   one drop of blues turning a paper clip
   into three wings and a bone into a revolt
you know
   a blues passing up the stereotype symbols
you know
   go into the dark meat of a crocodile
   and pin point the process
you know
   into a solo a hundred times
   like the first line of Aretha Franklin
you know
   like Big Mama Thornton
you know
   i sure would like to write a blues

you know
    if i could write me a blues
you know
    a blues that you could all feel at the same time
    on the same level like a Joe Louis punch
you know
    a punch that could break a computer
    into an event like Guinea Bissau
you know
    if i could write me a blues
you know
    a nice long blues
you know
    an up to the minute blues
you know
    a smack dab in the middle of depression blues
you know
    a blues without incidental music
you know
    without spending time being incidental
you know
    if i could write a blues
you know
    a blues without the popular use of the word love
you know
    without running love love love in the ground

you know
    a serious blues
you know
    a significant blues
you know
    an unsubmissive blues
you know
    a just because we exist blues
you know
    a blues
you know
    a terrible blues about the terrible terrible need
    i have to write the blues
you know
    if i could write a nice long blues
you know
    a nice long blues
you know
    it sure would feel good to my writing hand
you know
    you know
you know

LOOK FOR YOU YESTERDAY,
HERE YOU COME TODAY

Part of my charm:
>   envious blues feeling
>   separation of church & state
>   grim calls from drunk debutantes

Morning never aids me in my quest.
I have to trim my beard in solitude.
I try to hum lines from "The Poet In New York".

People saw metal all around the house on Saturdays.
>   The Phone rings.

terrible poems come in the mail. Descriptions of
>   celibate parties
>   torn trousers: Great Poets dying
>   with their strophes on. & me
>   incapable of a simple straightforward
>   anger.

It's so diffuse
being alive. Suddenly one is aware
>   that nobody really gives a damn.
>   My wife is pregnant with *her* child.
>   "It means nothing to me", sez Strindberg.

An avalanche of words
could cheer me up. Words from Great Sages.
Was James Karolis a great sage??
Why did I let Ora Matthews beat
him up
in the bathroom? Haven't I learned
my lesson.

I would take up painting
if I cd think of a way to do it
better than Leonardo. Than Bosch
Than Hogarth. Than Kline.

Frank walked off the stage, singing
"My silence is as important as Jack's incessant yatter."

I am a mean hungry sorehead.
Do I have the capacity for grace??

To arise one smoking spring
& find one's youth has taken off
for greener parts.

A sudden blankness in the day
as if there were no afternoon.
& all my piddling joys retreated
to their own dopey mythic worlds.

The hours of the atmosphere
grind their teeth like hags.

       (When will world war two be over?)

I stood up on a mailbox
waving my yellow tee-shirt
watching the gray tanks
stream up Central Ave.
              All these thots
              are Flowers Of Evil
              cold & lifeless
              as subway rails

the sun like a huge cobblestone
flaking its brown slow rays
primititi
         once, twice, . My life
         seems over & done with.
         Each morning I rise
         like a sleep walker
         & rot a little more.

All the lovely things I've known have disappeared.
I have all my pubic hair & am lonely.
There is probably no such place as Battle Creek,
    Michigan!

Tom Mix dead in a Boston Nightclub
before I realized what happened.

People laugh when I tell them about Dickie Dare!
What is one to do in an alien planet
where the people breath New Ports?
Where is my space helmet, I sent for it
3 lives ago . . . when there were box tops.

What has happened to box tops??

O, God . . . I must have a belt that glows green
in the dark. Where is my Captain Midnight decoder??
I can't understand what Superman is saying!

THERE *MUST* BE A LONE RANGER!!!

                    *   *   *

but this also
is part of my charm.
A maudlin nostalgia
that comes on
like terrible thoughts about death.

How dumb to be sentimental about anything
To call it love
& cry pathetically
into the long black handkerchief
of the years.

> "Look for you yesterday
> Here you come today
> Your mouth wide open
> But what you got to say?"

> —part of my charm

> old envious   blues feeling
> ticking like   a big cobblestone clock.

I hear the reel running out . . .
the spectators are impatient for popcorn:
It was only a selected short subject

F. Scott Charon
will soon be glad-handing me
like a legionaire

My silver bullets all gone
My black mask trampled in the dust

& Tonto way off in the hills
moaning like Bessie Smith.

108   AMIRI BARAKA (LEROI JONES)

BLUES

in the night
in my half hour
negro dreams
i hear voices knocking at the door
i see walls dripping screams up
and down the halls

                    won't someone open
the door for me? won't some
one schedule my sleep
and don't ask no questions?
noise.

      like when he took me to his
home away from home place
and i died the long sought after
death he'd planned for me.
Yeah, bessie he put in the bacon
and it overflowed the pot.
and two days later
when i was talking
i started to grin.
as everyone knows
i am still grinning.

SONIA SANCHEZ   109

BLUES HAIKUS

let me be yo wil
derness let me be yo wind
blowing you all day.

am i yo philly
outpost? man when you sail in
to my house, you docked.

this is not a fire
sale but i am in heat
each time i see ya.

i am you loving
my own shadow watching
this noontime butterfly.

legs wrapped around you
camera. action. tightshot.
this is not a rerun.

is there a fo rent
sign on my butt? you got no
territorial rights here.

when we say good-bye
i want yo tongue inside my
mouth dancing hello.

you too slippery
for me. can't hold you long or
hard. not enough nites.

SET. NO. 2

i've been keeping company, with the layaway man.
i say, i've been keeping company, with the layaway man.
each time he come by, we do it on the installment plan.

every Friday night, he comes walking up to me do'
i say, every Friday night, he comes walking up to me do'
empty pockets hanging, right on down to the floor.

gonna get me a man, who pays for it up front
i say, gonna get me a man, who pays for it up front
cuz when i needs it, can't wait til the middle of next
        month

i've been keeping company, with the layaway man
i say, i've been keeping company, with the layaway man
each time he come by, we do it on the installment plan
each time he come by, we do it on the installment plan

MASTER CHARGE BLUES

it's wednesday night baby
and i'm all alone
wednesday night baby
and i'm all alone
sitting with myself
waiting for the telephone

wanted you baby
but you said you had to go
wanted you yeah
but you said you had to go
called your best friend
but he can't come 'cross no more

did you ever go to bed
at the end of a busy day
look over and see the smooth
where your hump usta lay
feminine odor and no reason why
i said feminine odor and no reason why
asked the lord to help me
he shook his head "not i"

but i'm a modern woman baby
ain't gonna let this get me down
i'm a modern woman
ain't gonna let this get me down
gonna take my master charge
and get everything in town

INFLATION BLUES

Inflation blues is what we got.
Poah Black folks must do without.
Can't buy no bread, can't buy no house.
Can't live no better than a louse.

We useta sing way back when
Depression was and come again:
"What's the matter with Uncle Sam?
He took away my sugar; now he's messing with
    my ham."

A piece of beef too high to buy;
Chicken ain't no better.
Fatback and fish too high to fry;
A quarter mails one letter.

It useta be when I was small
Ten dollars bought enough for y'all.
My daddy couldn't make one trip
From corner store to carry all.

This morning Lawd, I bought one bag
And "fifteen dollars" sez that ole hag.
I swallowed hard and bit my lip.
That sho was one expensive trip.

The gas too high to fill the tank
One year cost more than did the car
Bus fare so high I gotta walk
Cost more to live than foreign war.

You can't afford to live or die.
A baby cost too much to buy.
Hospital bed for just one day
Will scare your very death away.

I don't know what we coming to
The Gov'ment say they gonna do.
And all they do is raise the rent
And talk again how much they spent.

The wheat, the corn, and other grain
If it is dry, or if it rain
Must go across the world to feed
While we must pay and still must need.

Our city streets are full of crime
With robbers, muggers, raping blind.
Poah people can't afford to sleep.
Your house ain't safe, and you can't sweep

Your troubles underneath the rug
'Cause then that bad old carpet bug
Will rot you down, your house and all
Don't care which way you try to crawl.

Inflation blues is what we got.
Poah Black folks must do without.
We naked in the wind and blind
As jaybirds in moulting time.

WOKE UP CRYING THE BLUES

woke up crying the blues
bore witness to the sadness of the day
the peaceful man from atlanta
was slaughtered yesterday
got myself together
drank in the sweetness of sunshine
wrote three poems to the peaceful lamb
from atlanta, made love to a raging black woman
drank wine, the grapes of poets
got high, saw angels
leading the lamb to heaven?—
the blues gonna get me, gonna get me
for sure, went to the beach too
forget, if only eye can about the gentle
soul from georgia, ate
clam chowder soup & fish sandwiches
made love in the sand to this same
beautiful woman
drank in all her sweet—
ness, lost future child in the sand
saw a bloody sun falling behind
weeping, purple clouds
as tears fell in a cloudburst of warm rain
for this dreaming lamb eye cant forget
the bloody moon-star, sinking

118

into the purple, cloud tossed grave
blackness falls through praying
hours of day, go out into
the decay of sunlight
copped three keys—
the key of creative joy
the key of happiness
the key of subliminal sadness—
came back on a whim to her house
which was disrupted, watched the gloom
on the idiot tube, kissed her in a panic
then spaced all the way home
by route of the mad
deathway, dropped tears in my lap
for the turning cheek from atlanta
come home safe at last—
two letters under the door
grips at the root of my being—
a love letter from the past shakes up
whatever is left of that memory
at last another poem published
good news during a bad news weekend—
lights out, drink of grapes
severed sight closes
another day in the life

QUINCY TROUPE   119

LETTER: BLUES

> *"Those Great Lake Winds*
> *blow all around:*
> *I'm a light-coat man*
> *in a heavy-coat town."*
>
> WARING CUNEY

Yellow freesia are like twining arms;
I'm buying shower curtains, smoke alarms,
And Washington, and you, Love—states away.
The clouds are flat. The sky is going grey.

I'm fiddling with the juice jug, honey pot,
White chrysanthemums that I just bought.
At home, there is a violet, 3-D moon
And pachysandra vines for me to prune,

And old men with checkered shirts, suspenders,
Paper bags and Cutty bottles, menders
Of frayed things and balding summer lawns,
Watching TV baseball, shelling prawns.

The women that we love! Their slit-eyed ways
Of telling us to mind, pop-eyed dismays.
We need these folks, each one of them. We do.
The insides of my wrists still ache with you.

Does the South watch over wandering ones
Under different moons and different suns?
I have my mother's copper ramekin,
A cigar box to keep your letters in.

At least the swirl ceilings are very high,
And the Super's rummy, sort of sly.
I saw a slate-branched tree sway from the roots—
I've got to buy some proper, winter boots.

So many boxes! Crates and crates of books.
I must get oil soap, bleach, and picture hooks.
A sidewalk crack in Washington, D.C.
Will feed my city dirt roots. Wait for me.

ELIZABETH ALEXANDER   121

CHEATING WOMAN BLUES HAIKU

In whipping noon sun,
a black snake dances through grass
to warm milk in bowls.

In biting noon sun,
a black snake dances through grass
to warm milk in bowls.

Daisies in her hair,
my woman crosses the tracks
to another man.

Cuttin' trees all day,
sweat and sawdust in my eyes;
she thinks I can't see.

Cuttin' trees all day,
sweat and sawdust cloud my eyes;
she thinks I can't see.

In a field of grass,
she lays her head down to dream
of muddy waters.

FEELING FUCKED/UP

Lord she's gone done left me done packed/up
        and split
and I with no way to make her
come back and everywhere the world is bare
bright bone white   crystal sand glistens
dope death dead dying and jiving drove
her away made her take her laughter and her smiles
and her softness and her midnight sighs—

Fuck Coltrane and music and clouds drifting in the sky
fuck the sea and trees and the sky and birds
and alligators and all the animals that roam the earth
fuck marx and mao fuck fidel and nkrumah and
democracy and communism fuck smack and pot
and red ripe tomatoes fuck joseph fuck mary fuck
god jesus and all the disciples fuck fanon nixon
and malcolm fuck the revolution fuck freedom fuck
the whole muthafucking thing
all i want now is my woman back
so my soul can sing

FACING OFF

Blues in my meal barrel,
     and there's blues up on my shelf—
and there's blues in my bed
     'cause I'm sleeping by myself.

MERLINE JOHNSON
Blues Everywhere (1937)

Now you must want your mama
     to lay down and die for you—
layin' down is all right,
     but dyin' will never do!

HOCIEL THOMAS
Deep Water Blues (1926)
BY ROBERT BROWN (WASHBOARD SAM)

THE BLUES

These are the blues:
a longing beyond control
left on an unwelcome doorstep,
slipping in when the door is opened.

These are the blues:
a lonely woman crouched at a bar,
gulping a blaze of Scotch and rye,
using a tear for a chaser.

The blues are fears that
blossom like ragweeds
in a well-kept bed of roses.

(Nobody knows how tired I am.
And there ain't a soul who gives a damn.)

MARRIED BLUES

I didn't want it, you wanted it.
Now you've got it you don't like it.
You can't get out of it now.

Pork and beans, diapers to wash,
Too poor for the movies, too tired to love.
There's nothing we can do.

Hot stenographers on the subway.
The grocery boy's got a big one.
We can't do anything about it.

You're only young once.
You've got to go when your time comes.
That's how it is. Nobody can change it.

Guys in big cars whistle.
Freight trains moan in the night.
We can't get away with it.

That's the way life is.
Everybody's in the same fix.
It will never be any different.

LONESOME BOY BLUES

Oh nobody's a long time
Nowhere's a big pocket
To put little
Pieces of nice things that

Have never really happened

To anyone except
Those people who were lucky enough
Not to get born
Oh lonesome's a bad place

To get crowded into

With only
Yourself riding back and forth
On
A blind white horse
Along an empty road meeting
All your
Pals face to face

Nobody's a long time

KENNETH PATCHEN   129

CONCENTRATION CAMP BLUES

I aint jokin people, I aint playin around
Wouldnt jive you people, aint playin around
They got the Indian on the reservation
                    got us in the ghetto town

Like when you down home, tryin to get out
A mule in his stall trying to kick out
You gets to it in the ghetto but you aint got out

Wouldnt jive you people, this a natural fact
They watchin us all people, a natural fact
The man is plannin to put a harness on my back

So get with it people, let's get outa his camp
I aint jokin, I got to get outa his camp
Cause the man is ready to number us all with a
    rubber stamp

OUTER SPACE BLUES
To Sun Ra Myth

People, I heard the news the other day
                    like to scared me half to death
Yeah things happen in this world
                    like to scared me half to death
TV say a spaceship is comin here
                    if it do wont be no people left

But I tell you folks, spaceship cant be so bad
Reckon I just a fool people,
                    spaceship cant be too bad
I been on earth all my life,
                    and all my life I been mad

So when the spaceship land
                    I aint runnin too fast
I say, I reckon I might not run too fast
I might run over into Mississippi
                    and you know I can't pass

Hold it people, I see a flying saucer comin
                    guess I wait and see
Yeah, a spaceship comin
                    guess I wait and see
All I know they might look just like me

BLUES

Those five or six young guys
hunched on the stoop
that oven-hot summer night
whistled me over. Nice
and friendly. So, I stop.
MacDougal or Christopher
Street in chains of light.

A summer festival. Or some
saint's. I wasn't too far from
home, but not too bright
for a nigger, and not too dark.
I figured we were all
one, wop, nigger, jew,
besides, this wasn't Central Park.
I'm coming on too strong? You figure
right! They beat this yellow nigger
black and blue.

Yeah. During all this, scared
in case one used a knife,
I hung my olive-green, just-bought
sports coat on a fire plug.
I did nothing. They fought
each other, really. Life

gives them a few kicks,
that's all. The spades, the spicks.

My face smashed in, my bloody mug
pouring, my olive-branch jacket saved
from cuts and tears,
I crawled four flights upstairs.
Sprawled in the gutter, I
remember a few watchers waved
loudly, and one kid's mother shouting
like "Jackie" or "Terry,"
"now that's enough!"
It's nothing really.
They don't get enough love.

You know they wouldn't kill
you. Just playing rough,
like young America will.
Still, it taught me something
about love. If it's so tough,
forget it.

RESERVATION BLUES

Dancing all alone, feeling nothing good
It's been so long since someone understood
All I've seen is, is why I weep
And all I had for dinner was some sleep

You know I'm lonely, I'm so lonely
My heart is empty and I've been so hungry
All I need for my hunger to ease
Is anything that you can give me please

[chorus:]
I ain't got nothing, I heard no good news
I fill my pockets with those reservation blues
Those old, those old rez blues, those old reservation
    blues
And if you ain't got choices
What else do you choose?

[repeat chorus twice]

And if you ain't got choices
Ain't got much to lose

BILINGUAL BLUES

Soy un ajiaco de contradicciones.
I have mixed feelings about everything.
Name your tema, I'll hedge;
name your cerca, I'll straddle it
like a cubano.

I have mixed feelings about everything.
Soy un ajiaco de contradicciones.
Vexed, hexed, complexed,
hyphenated, oxygenated, illegally alienated,
psycho soy, cantando voy:
You say tomato,
I say tu madre;
You say potato,
I say Pototo.
Let's call the hole
un hueco, the thing
a cosa, and if the cosa goes into the hueco,
consider yourself en casa,
consider yourself part of the family.

Soy un ajiaco de contradicciones,
un puré de impurezas:
a little square from Rubik's Cuba
que nadie nunca acoplará.
(Cha–cha–chá.)

GUSTAVO PÉREZ FIRMAT   135

BLUES ON YELLOW

The canary died in the gold mine, her dreams got lost
    in the sieve.
The canary died in the gold mine, her dreams got lost
    in the sieve.
Her husband the crow killed under the railroad, the
    spokes hath shorn his wings.

Something's cookin' in Chin's kitchen, ten thousand
    yellow-bellied sapsuckers baked in a pie.
Something's cookin' in Chin's kitchen, ten thousand
    yellow-bellied sapsuckers baked in a pie.
Something's cookin in Chin's kitchen, die die yellow
    bird, die die.

O crack an egg on the griddle, yellow will ooze into white.
O crack an egg on the griddle, yellow will ooze into white.
Run, run, sweet little Puritan, yellow will ooze into white.

If you cut my yellow wrists, I'll teach my yellow toes to
    write.
If you cut my yellow wrists, I'll teach my yellow toes to
    write.
If you cut my yellow fists, I'll teach my yellow feet to
    fight.

Do not be afraid to perish, my mother, Buddha's
   compassion is nigh.
Do not be afraid to perish, my mother, our boat will
   sail tonight.
Your babies will reach the promised land, the stars will
   be their guide.

I am so mellow yellow, mellow yellow, Buddha sings in
   my veins.
I am so mellow yellow, mellow yellow, Buddha sings in
   my veins.
O take me to the land of the unreborn, there's no life on
   earth without pain.

BLUE

As through marble or the lining of
certain fish split open and scooped
clean, this is the blue vein
that rides, where the flesh is even
whiter than the rest of her, the splayed
thighs mother forgets, busy struggling
for command over bones: her own,
those of the chaise longue, all
equally uncooperative, and there's
the wind, too. This is her hair, gone
from white to blue in the air.

This is the black, shot with blue, of my dark
daddy's knuckles, that do not change, ever.
Which is to say they are no more pale
in anger than at rest, or when, as
I imagine them now, they follow
the same two fingers he has always used
to make the rim of every empty blue
glass in the house sing.
Always, the same
blue-to-black sorrow
no black surface can entirely hide.

Under the night, somewhere
between the white that is nothing so much as
blue, and the black that is, finally, nothing,
I am the man neither of you remembers.
Shielding, in the half-dark,
the blue eyes I sometimes forget
I don't have. Pulling my own stoop-
shouldered kind of blues across paper.
Apparently misinformed about the rumored
stuff of dreams: everywhere I inquired,
I was told look for blue.

DEEP SONG
For B.H.

The blues calling my name.
She is singing a deep song.
She is singing a deep song.
I am human.
He calls me crazy.
He says, "You must be
crazy."
I say, "Yes, I'm crazy."
He sits with his knees apart.
His fly is broken.
She is singing a deep song.
He smiles.
She is singing a deep song.
"Yes, I'm crazy."
I care about you.
I care.
I care about you.
I care.
He lifts his eyebrows.
The blues is calling my name.
I tell him he'd better
do something about his fly.
He says something softly.
He says something so softly

that I can't even hear him.
He is a dark man.
Sometimes he is a good dark man.
Sometimes he is a bad dark man.
I love him.

SOLEDAD

I smell water and I hear God knocking.
The way I feel tonight
The stars could be my mother's eyes
And go out and I wouldn't care.

People I eat music.
But sometimes I get weak
From laughing to myself and her face
Fades like a stranger's
And only the dusk reminds me of her lips.

I circle the night trying to ambush
The sky and closing my eyes No
Is the only word I hear.
It hurts to recall the origin of that echo.

As I retreat from the sound
And my soul leaks
My nose raw and open wide as Fifth Avenue
I wound easy
But in solitude I hum a bebop blues.

Listen someone's banging
And is it the rain?
She rode so smooth I soon forgot
My wild horse.
O Angela I rode my hearse into a lake!

SOME PIECES

When two elephants fight
It's only the grass that suffers

In the land of nod
Coke is king and scag god

I'm going I'm gone
Baby look what you've done
Left me and now day has come

The statues of some people never smile
Buddha does like a senile grandmother

Between us the bread was always stale

Should I lay my head on railroad tracks
Or should I lay my head on your wide lap

They can't plow the river
Snow lies on everything except
The road and it's black black

If I were a catfish swimming
In the deep blue sea
I'd start all you women
Jumping in after me

Somebody's in my bed
And they got my long johns on
I don't mind you taking my woman
But you better take my long johns off

And the white hand
Which bought me here
Which I learnt to hold
Now pushes me off the cliff

You can go home now

Your fingers are negroes
They do all the work for your fat arms

BROOM SONG

O broom tell me,
who has danced your blues
as well as me?
Pray tell whose hands
have held you as gingerly.

Who has endured the doors
you've shut so tightly against me
opened only out of necessity?

How often I've tried
to flee your dumbing dance
to find only you there—
my one-last-chance.

Tell me O broom,
old friend—so often my refuge
or reason for the wrongs
who has danced this blues
as well as we, for as long?

SICKNESS BLUES

Lord Lord I got the sickness blues, I must've done
     something wrong
There ain't no Lord to call on, now my youth is gone

Sickness blues, don't want to screw no more
Sickness blues, can't get it up no more
Tears come in my eyes, feel like an old tired whore

I went to see the doctor, he shot me with poison germs
I got out of the hospital, my head was full of worms

All I can think is Death, father's getting old
He can't walk half a block, his feet feel cold

I went down to Santa Fe take vacation there
Indians selling turquoise in dobe huts in Taos Pueblo
     Square
Got headache in La Fonda, I could get sick anywhere

Must be my bad karma, making these pretty boys
Hungry ghosts chasing me, because I been chasing
     joys
Lying here in bed alone, playing with my toys

I musta been doing something wrong meat &
    cigarettes
Bow down before my lord, 100 thousand regrets
All my poems down in hell, that's what pride begets

Sick and angry, lying in my hospital bed
Doctor Doctor bring morphine before I'm totally dead
Sick and angry at the national universe O my aching
    head

Someday I'm gonna get out of here, go somewhere
    alone
Yeah I'm going to leave this town with noise of rattling
    bone
I got the sickness blues, you'll miss me when I'm gone

Boulder, July 19, 1975

BAD MOTHER BLUES

When you were arrested, child, and I had to take your
    pocketknife
When you were booked and I had to confiscate your
    pocketknife
It had blood on it from where you'd tried to take
    your life

It was the night before Thanksgiving, all the family
    coming over
The night before Thanksgiving, all the family coming
    over
We had to hide your porno magazine and put your
    handcuffs undercover

Each naked man looked at you, said, Baby who do you
    think you are
Each man looked straight down on you, like a waiting
    astronomer's star
Solely, disgustedly, each wagged his luster

I've decided to throw horror down the well and wish
    on it
Decided I'll throw horror down the well and wish on it
And up from the water will shine my sweet girl in her
    baby bonnet

A thief will blind you with his flashlight
                                but a daughter be your bouquet
A thief will blind you with his flashlight
                                but a daughter be your bouquet
When the thief's your daughter you turn your eyes the
        other way

I'm going into the sunflower field where all of them are
        facing me
I'm going into the sunflower field so all of them are
        facing me
Going to go behind the sunflowers, feel all the sun that
        I can't see

RAMBLING
in Lewisburg Prison

In general population, census
is consensus—ain't nowhere to run
to in these walls, walls like a mind—
we visitors stand in a yellow circle
so the tower can frisk us with light,
finger the barrels on thirsty rifles.

I got rambling, got rambling on my mind.

In general population, madness runs
swift through the river changing, changing
in hearts, men tacked in their chairs,
resigned to hope we weave into air,
talking this and talking that and one brutha
asks "Tell us how to get these things
they got, these houses, these cars.
We want the real revolution." Things . . .

I got rambling, got rambling on my mind.

In the yellow circle the night stops
like a boy shot running from a Ruger 9mm
carrying .44 magnum shells, a sista
crying in the glass booth to love's law,
to violence of backs bent over to the raw
libido of men, cracking, cracking, crack . . .

I got rambling, got rambling on my mind.

UNCLE BULL-BOY

His brother   after dinner
once a year would play the piano
short and tough in white shirt
plaid suspenders   green tie and
checked trousers.
Two teeth were gold.   His eyes
were pink with alcohol.   His fingers
thumped for Auld Lang Syne.
He played St. Louis Woman
Boogie, Blues, the light
pedestrian.

        But one night   after dinner
after chitterlings and pigs' feet
after bourbon rum and rye
after turnip greens and mustard greens
and sweet potato pie
Bullboy looking everywhere
realized his brother was not there.

Who would emphasize the luxury
of ice cream by the gallon who would
repeat effusively the glamor not the gall
of five degrees outstanding on the wall?
Which head would nod and then recall

the crimes   the apples stolen from the stalls
the soft coal stolen by the pile?
Who would admire
the eighteenth pair of forty
dollar shoes?
Who could extol their mother with good
brandy as his muse?

His brother   dead from drinking
Bullboy drank to clear his thinking
saw the roach inside the riddle.
Soon the bubbles from his glass
were the only bits of charm
which overcame his folded arms.

GET AWAY 1928
For Martin Sewell

Pack up and hit it
Road warrior got the
Big one

Like the Dipper
Urban area—a trip
Far gone

Click the dusty boots
separated troops
Movin' on
Movin' on

Take him off the farm
Seen the Parée
Uh Huh

Hard to "yes, boss"
After francophillic
got some

Brothers swung low
Belles chimed
Sweet french quiches

"Boy" in the US
All man to
parisians

Scared the Crow
Plot-condemned—no way
couldn't keep him

Flee to the
steel belt (work-related
health reasons).

Rusty got the clay
still baked to his
pained face

Collard green and hoe cake
withdrawl from his
momma's place

Foul hawk breezing through
with the Negro
northern news

you ain't never far away
enough to not need
the blues.

TRACIE MORRIS   155

JOE CHAPPEL'S FOOT LOG BOTTOM
BLUES 1952

I left that bottle at the Blue Moon.
Emptied the bottle at the Blue Moon.
And I'm gone see my woman soon.

She lives in a shack with a chicken yard and coop.
Got to be quiet—don't wake them hens sleep in the coop.
To get in that shack gone have to bow, scrape and stoop.
Oh, I say I'm gone have to bow, scrape and stoop.

I need a taste more—gone stop by Bobby's for a sip.
Needed a taste more so stopped by Bobby's for a sip.
Now, Lord, it's done come up a cloud mighty quick.

Clouds done moved in quick and filled up this room.
Clouds done come and covered up the stars and moon;
I expect, it's gone come down a rain awful soon.

Got to cross Ten Yard Branch to the other side.
Got to cross the branch to the Choiceville side.
I just tripped over a root and damn near died.

Here I am stumbling—drunk off some liquor.
I say, I'm stumbling drunk from stump liquor.
Going to see my woman—Lord, all we do is bicker.

My troubles fill a pail faster than this rain coming
    down.
Said, troubles overflow faster than rain coming down.
Lord, lightning shined them raindrops like gems in
    your crown.
Lord, she a good and beautiful woman like a jewel in
    your crown.

These foot logs getting slapped and kissed by the
    rising branch.
I said, foot logs kissed and slapped by the rising
    branch.
Lord, hope I can get across and she lift that latch.

SWING SHIFT BLUES

What is better than leaving a bar
in the middle of the afternoon
besides staying in it or else not
having gone into it in the first place
because you had a decent woman to be with?
The air smells particularly fresh
after the stale beer and piss smells.
You can stare up at the whole sky:
it's blue and white and does not
stare back at you like the bar mirror,
and there's What's-'is-name coming out
right behind you saying, "I don't
believe it, I don't believe it: there
he is, staring up at the fucking sky
with his mouth open. Don't
you realize, you stupid son of a bitch,
that it is a quarter to four
and we have to clock in in
fifteen minutes to go to work?"
So we go to work and do no work
and can even breathe in the Bull's face
because he's been into the other bar
that we don't go to when he's there.

THE BLUES

Much of what is said here
must be said twice,
a reminder that no one
takes an immediate interest in the pain of others.

Nobody will listen, it would seem,
if you simply admit
your baby left you early this morning
she didn't even stop to say good-bye.

But if you sing it again
with the help of the band
which will now lift you to a higher,
more ardent and beseeching key,

people will not only listen;
they will shift to the sympathetic
edges of their chairs,
moved to such acute anticipation

by that chord and the delay that follows,
they will not be able to sleep
unless you release with one finger
a scream from the throat of your guitar

and turn your head back to the microphone
to let them know
you're a hard-hearted man
but that woman's sure going to make you cry.

FIGURES

No, de blues ain't nothin'
But a good man feelin' bad.

TRADITIONAL

The blues ain't nothin'
But a bad woman feelin' good.

TRADITIONAL

ANY WOMAN'S BLUES

every woman is a victim of the feel blues, too.

Soft lamp shinin
        and me alone in the night.
Soft lamp is shinin
        and me alone in the night.
Can't take no one beside me
        need mo'n jest some man to set me right.

I left many peoples and places
        tryin not to be alone.
Left many a person and places
        I lived my life alone.
I need to get myself together.
        Yes, I need to make myself to home.

What's gone can be a window
        a circle in the eye of the sun.
What's gone can be a window
        a circle, well, in the eye of the sun.
Take the circle from the world, girl,
        you find the light have gone.

These is old blues
        and I sing em like any woman do.
These the old blues
        and I sing em, sing em, sing em. Just like any
                woman do.
My life ain't done yet.
        Naw. My song ain't through.

I'M A FOOL TO LOVE YOU

Some folks will tell you the blues is a woman,
Some type of supernatural creature.
My mother would tell you, if she could,
About her life with my father,
A strange and sometimes cruel gentleman.
She would tell you about the choices
A young black woman faces.
Is falling in with some man
A deal with the devil
In blue terms, the tongue we use
When we don't want nuance
To get in the way,
When we need to talk straight?
My mother chooses my father
After choosing a man
Who was, as we sing it,
Of no account.
This man made my father look good,
That's how bad it was.
He made my father seem like an island
In the middle of a stormy sea,
He made my father look like a rock.
And is the blues the moment you realize
You exist in a stacked deck,
You look in a mirror at your young face,

The face my sister carries,
And you know it's the only leverage
You've got?
Does this create a hurt that whispers
How you going to do?
Is the blues the moment
You shrug your shoulders
And agree, a girl without money
Is nothing, dust
To be pushed around by any old breeze?
Compared to this,
My father seems, briefly,
To be a fire escape.
This is the way the blues works
Its sorry wonders,
Makes trouble look like
A feather bed,
Makes the wrong man's kisses
A healing.

MUDDY WATERS & THE
CHICAGO BLUES

Good news from the windy city: Thomas Edison's
Time on the planet has been validated. The guitars
And harps begin their slow translation
Of the street, an S.O.S. of what you need
And what you have. The way this life
Tries to roar you down, you have to fight

Fire with fire: the amplified power
Of a hip rotating in an upstairs flat
Vs. the old indignities; the static
Heat of *nothing, nowhere,*

No how against this conversation
Of fingers and tongues, this
Rent party above the
Slaughter-house.

LEADBELLY

You can actually hear it in his voice:
Sometimes the only way to discuss it
Is to grip a guitar as if it were
Somebody's throat
And pluck. If there were

A ship off of this planet,
An ark where the blues could show
Its other face,

A street where you could walk,
Just walk without dogged air at
Your heels, at your back, don't
You think he'd choose it?
Meanwhile, here's the tune:
Bad luck, empty pockets,
Trouble walking your way
With his tin ear.

LANGSTON HUGHES

LANGSTON HUGHES
LANGSTON HUGHES
    O come now
    & sang
them weary blues—

Been tired here
feelin' low down
    Real
    tired here
since you quit town

Our ears no longer trumpets
Our mouths no more bells
    FAMOUS POET©——
    Busboy—Do tell
us of hell—

Mr. Shakespeare in Harlem
Mr. Theme for English B
    Preach on
    kind sir
of death, if it please—

We got no more promise
We only got ain't
        Let us in
        on how
you 'came a saint

LANGSTON
LANGSTON
        LANGSTON HUGHES
        Won't you send
all heaven's news

SONG FOR LANGSTON

I sang all night
And cried all day

Been waitin' for a
Storm to come my way

Drown the tears
Make soft the pain

I hope my prayers
Are not in vain

MUDDY WATERS
For Jerry Ward

He
put a moving in my father.
I
saw it ripe as liver
hung
up
on hog
killing day.
And they made
the image they dreamed
from it.
I
saw gods in their strides,
feisty bold, desires tilted
like derby hats. As
they made
space. He
put a moving in my father.
I
saw him down
on his spirit/breathing
legends into brown eyes.
Jump
joy

roots of sudden power.
Mixed
tastes of green 'simmons
and garlic.

To suck groans from smiles.
As
they pocketed the meaning
in their genes and
kept evil out
side vows in their dance.
Turned
quietness to flames in loins.
Shocked
segregated fingers
to clenched fists.
As
men paraded.
They
left shadows of lynchings and
made images.
Hung
them above creation
to drip
on generations.

He
put a moving in my father

BIG MAMA THORNTON

They call me Big Mama and I make
much music when I walk. I know
you want to find the easy way
down to these marrow-full bones,
but please don't mess me over.
Don't play me like a puppy, lick
my face then bark at me. Do
and the two-headed lady gone
have your address and your
unlisted phone number.

I weigh three hundred pounds
and all this is real, baby. Ain't
nobody else living with me in this plush
house of mine. This just some deep
country meat padding your ride.

They call me Big Mama and the ground
be strumming stones.
These fine hamhocks will knock
your black iron pot all night long
but please don't mess me over.
Don't play me like a puppy, lick
my face then bark at me. Do
and I'll cut you so smooth,
I'll be on that train to Chicago
before you even start to bleed.

POEM ALMOST WHOLLY IN MY OWN MANNER

Where the Southern cross the Yellow Dog
In Moorhead, Mississippi,
                my mother sheltered her life out

In Leland, a few miles down US 82,
                unfretted and unaware,
Layered between history and a three-line lament

About to be brought forth
                on the wrong side of the tracks
All over the state and the Deep South.

We all know what happened next,
                blues and jazz and rhythm-and-blues,
Then rock-and-roll, then sex-and-drugs-and-rock-
    and-roll, lick by lick

Blowing the lanterns out—and everything else—
    along the levees:
Cotton went west, the music went north
                and everywhere in between,

Time, like a burning wheel, scorching along by the
    highway side,
Reorganizing, relayering,
                turning the tenants out.

———————

9 p.m. August sky eleemosynary, such sweet grief,
Music the distant thunder chord
                              that shudders our lives.
Black notes. The black notes
That follow our footsteps like blood from a cut finger.
                                        Like that.

Fireflies, slow angel eyes,
                        nod and weave,
Tracking our chary attitudes, our malevolent mercies.

Charity, sometimes, we have,
                            appearing and disappearing
Like stars when nightwash rises through us.

(Hope and faith we lip-sync,
                        a dark dharma, a goat grace,
A grace like rain, that goes where rain goes.)

Discreetly the evening enters us,
                            overwhelms us,
As out here whatever lifts, whatever lowers, intersects.

———————

Interstices. We live in the cracks.
Under Ezekiel and his prophesies,
                              under the wheel.

Poetry's what's left between the lines—
                    a strange speech and a hard language,
It's all in the unwritten, it's all in the unsaid . . .

And that's a comfort, I think,
                              for our lack and inarticulation.
For our scalded flesh and our singed hair.

But what would Robert Johnson say,
                    hell-hounded and brimstone-tongued?
What would W. C. Handy say,

Those whom the wheel has overturned,
                              those whom the fire has,
And the wind has, unstuck and unstrung?

They'd say what my mother said—
                    a comfort, perhaps, but too cold
Where the Southern cross the Yellow Dog.

DREAM SONG [no. 40]

I'm scared a lonely. Never see my son,
easy be not to see anyone,
combers out to sea
know they're goin somewhere but not me.
Got a little poison, got a little gun,
I'm scared a lonely.

I'm scared a only one thing, which is me,
from othering I don't take nothin, see,
for any hound dog's sake.
But this is where I livin, where I rake
my leaves and cop my promise, this' where we
cry oursel's awake.

Wishin was dyin but I gotta make
it all this way to that bed on these feet
where peoples said to meet.
Maybe but even if I see my son
forever never, get back on the take,
free, black & forty-one.

JOHN BERRYMAN LISTENING TO ROBERT JOHNSON'S *KING OF THE DELTA BLUES*, JANUARY 1972

Am I a dead man? Am I a dead man?
—Hards to say, Mr. Bones, could be.
I think some hellhound's got the scent of me.
Hear him, I do, often.
He stands like Henry's father in the black room
Filled with light. Henry's childhood home.

And Henry, like him, is undone,
Conjuring him, conjuring him.
Mad Robert Johnson did traffic with ghosts,
Which hurt themselves, coming to their lifes again.
—Why, now, Sir Bones, you messin' wif' dem?
Henry's terrible lost,

Though Henry has lived, longer by much
Than Robert Johnson, who met the devil at a crossroads,
Dead at 26.
Hellhound, truly, *do* exist.
And Henry will not sing more, either. He loads
The gin with ice cube, lemon twist.

DAVID WOJAHN   179

ARRIVAL

They say Robert Johnson couldn't play that guitar
        one lick
until he gave his soul away, and that his voice near itched.
Folks became amazed by the music he could make,
                                        once they listened.

Looking at birds, my friend can see the dinosaurs they
        were.
They scare her winging down. She can't decide the sound.

They say before he was cursed to live on his belly, give up
                        the terrible wings, Lucifer was loved.
They say that night he became a black man offering
                        vision, a faithful woman, then fame,
        and each time Johnson refused. His life was more
                                than half over, he could tell.

I believe insight doesn't happen at once.
I believe we ready ourselves that one more time and look
        differently, and change happens with small sights
        which accrete and feather. We see, we become.

When Alice and KwanLam were married, red-winged
        blackbirds came
from all over the grove, making the bamboo whish.

NOT GUILTY

The days are dog-eared, the edges torn,
ragged—like those pages
I ripped once out of library books,

for their photos
of Vallejo and bootless Robert Johnson.
A fine needs paying now

it's true, but
not by me.
I am no more guilty

than that thrush is
who sits there stripping moss
off the wet bark of a tree.

A red fleck, like his, glows
at the back of my head—a beauty mark,
left by the brain's after-jets.

I would not wish for the three brains
Robert required
to double-clutch his guitar

and chase those sounds he had to know
led down
and into a troubled dusky river, always.

Three brains did Johnson no earthly good,
neither his nor Vallejo's 4 & $\frac{1}{2}$
worked right exactly—O bunglers,

O banged-up pans of disaster!
Crying for days, said Cesar, & singing for months.
How can I be so strong some times,

at others weak? I wish to be free,
but free to do what? To leave myself behind?
To switch channels remotely?

Better to sing.
Not like the bird, but as they sang,
Cesar & Robert—

with the shocked & seeded
sweetness of an apple
split open by a meat cleaver.

BULOSAN LISTENS TO A RECORDING OF ROBERT JOHNSON

You sing a hard blues,
black man. You too have been driven:
a tumbleweed in strong wind.
I close my eyes, your voice rolls
out of the delta, sliding
over flashy chords
that clang like railroad tracks.

Gotta keep movin'
Gotta keep movin'
Hellhound on my trail

One summer
I worked the *wash-lye*
section of a cannery up north,
scrubbed schools of headless fish,
breathed ammonia fumes so fierce
I almost floated off
like the arm of a friend,
chopped clean at the elbow
by a cutter's machine.

Gotta keep movin'
Gotta keep movin'

We are the blue men, *Cabayan*,
our pockets empty of promise.
Mississippi, California—
bad luck conspires against us,
cheap wine stings in our veins.
We reel, drunk and bitter,
under the white, legal sun.
Robert Johnson/Carlos Bulosan—
our names so different,
our song the same.

FREIGHT

When a woman gets the blues
    she hangs her head and cries
But when a man gets the blues
    he hops a freight train and rides.

TRADITIONAL

THE BLUES DON'T CHANGE

> *"Now I'll tell you about the Blues.*
> *All Negroes like Blues. Why?*
> *Because they was born with the Blues.*
> *And now everybody have the Blues.*
> *Sometimes they don't know what it is."*
>
> LEADBELLY

And I was born with you, wasn't I, Blues?
Wombed with you, wounded, reared and forwarded
from address to address, stamped, stomped
and returned to sender by nobody else but you,
Blue Rider, writing me off every chance you
got, you mean old grudgeful-hearted, table-
turning demon, you, you sexy soul-sucking gem.

Blue diamond in the rough, you *are* forever.
You can't be outfoxed don't care how they cut
and smuggle and shine you on, you're like a
shadow, too dumb and stubborn and necessary
to let them turn you into what you ain't
with color or theory or powder or paint.

That's how you can stay in style without sticking
and not getting stuck. You know how to sting
where I can't scratch, and you move from frying

pan to skillet the same way you move people
to go to wiggling their boodies, juggling their
limbs, loosening that goose, upping their voices,
opening their pores, rolling their hips and lips.

They can shake their boodies but they can't shake *you*.

CINDERELLA

Seems like some people never get the blues
without Billie Holiday turned up loud
quart of Chivas at their feet—maybe Dewars
cigar   cigarette smoke   cat piss   dark rooms
their man two or three years late coming home
their woman packed up   out of town two days
rotten job no job   either way   no money
some people got to go to school to feel
what I feel every morning every night
I wake up wondering what new shit's coming
to make me wish I had yesterday back
I go to bed wondering how long I'll sleep
before something wakes me—siren, bad dream
I hear them   singing to themselves all night
their lives just turning bad   mine been that way

G. E. PATTERSON   189

ANNABELLE

My head hangs.
It's all to do with
a woman back in Alabama.
All to do with Annabelle
hugging every road sign
between here & Austin, Texas.
All to do with rope & blood.

He's all to do with America.
All to do with all the No-Dick
Joneses. Mornings shattered.
Crickets mourn—
sing out of genetic code.

All to do with shadows
kneeling in the woods.
All to do with inherited iron maidens.
Beg for death in the womb.
Beg for it inside skulls—flower,
dust, lilac perfume, cold fire.

Gonna get lowdown tonight.

FOR YOU, SWEETHEART, I'LL SELL
PLUTONIUM REACTORS

For you, sweetheart, I'll ride back down
into black smoke early Sunday morning
cutting fog, grab the moneysack
of gold teeth. Diamond mines
soil creep groan ancient cities, archaeological
diggings, & yellow bulldozers turn around all night
in blood-lit villages. Inhabitants here once gathered
        seashells
that glimmered like pearls. When the smoke clears,
        you'll see
an erected throne like a mountain to scale,
institutions built with bones, guns hidden in walls
that swing open like big-mouthed B-52s.
Your face in the mirror is my face. You tapdance
on tabletops for me, while corporate bosses
arm wrestle in back rooms for your essential downfall.
I entice homosexuals into my basement butcher shop.
I put my hands around another sharecropper's throat
for that mink coat you want from Saks Fifth,
short-change another beggarwoman,
steal another hit song from Sleepy
John Estes, salt another gold mine in Cripple Creek,
drive another motorcycle up a circular ice wall,
face another public gunslinger like a bad chest wound,

just to slide hands under black silk.
Like the Ancient Mariner steering a skeleton ship
against the moon, I'm their hired gunman
if the price is right, take a contract on myself.
They'll name mountains & rivers in my honor.
I'm a drawbridge over manholes for you, sweetheart.
I'm paid two hundred grand
to pick up a red telephone anytime & call up God.
I'm making tobacco pouches out of the breasts of
        Indian maidens
so we can stand in a valley & watch grass grow.

WOMAN, I GOT THE BLUES

I'm sporting a floppy existential sky-blue hat
when we meet in the Museum of Modern Art.

Later, we hold each other
with a gentleness that would break open
ripe fruit. Then we slow-drag
to Little Willie John, we bebop
to Bird LPs, bloodfunk, lungs paraphrased
till we break each other's fall.
For us there's no reason the scorpion
has to become our faith healer.

Sweet Mercy, I worship
the curvature of your ass.
I build an altar in my head.
I kiss your breasts & forget my name.

Woman, I got the blues.
Our shadows on floral wallpaper
struggle with cold-blooded mythologies.
But there's a stillness in us
like the tip of a magenta mountain.
Half-naked on the living-room floor;
the moon falling through the window
on you like a rapist.

Your breath's a dewy flower stalk
leaning into sweaty air.

HARD-LUCK RESUME

Thirteen persons once sat at my table.
Year before last I heard thunder in winter.
Often I take the last piece of cake
and leave knife and fork crosswise on my plate.
I wear old clothes on Easter Sunday.
My hobbies include sitting sideways on graves.
I put on my left shoe ahead of my right.
I walk in the front door and leave by the back.
I sneeze on request between midnight and noon.
I take off the ring from my best friend's finger.
I married three times, it was always in May.
I stumble in the morning
and when beginning a journey.

GONE AWAY BLUES

Sirs, when you are in your last extremity,
When your admirals are drowning in the grass-green sea,
When your generals are preparing the total
    catastrophe—
I just want you to know how you can not count on me.

  I have ridden to hounds through my ancestral halls,
  I have picked the eternal crocus on the ultimate hill,
  I have fallen through the window of the highest room,
  But don't ask me to help you 'cause I never will.

Sirs, when you move that map-pin how many souls must
    dance?
I don't think all those soldiers have died by happenstance.
The inscrutable look on your scrutable face I can read at
    a glance—
And I'm cutting out of here at the first chance.

  I have been wounded climbing the second stair,
  I have crossed the ocean in the hull of a live wire,
  I have eaten the asphodel of the dark side of the moon,
  But you can call me all day and I just won't hear.

O patriotic mister with your big ear to the ground,
Sweet old curly scientist wiring the birds for sound,

O lady with the Steuben glass heart and your heels so
    rich and round—
I'll send you a picture postcard from somewhere I can't
    be found.

I have discovered the grammar of the Public Good,
I have invented a language that *can* be understood,
I have found the map of where the body is hid,
And I won't be caught dead in *your* neighborhood.

O hygienic inventor of the bomb that's so clean,
O lily white Senator from East Turnip Green,
O celestial mechanic of the money machine—
I'm going someplace where *nobody* makes your scene.

Good-by, good-by, good-by,
Adios, au 'voir, so long,
Sayonara, dosvedanya, ciao,
By-by, by-by, by-by.

BROKEN BACK BLUES

O yr facing reality now—
& yr in the same beat groove—
you try to get up—
& find you just can't moo-oove
                              (take it take it

uncle john
we can play it all nite long...

          I got them things in my head—
no sounds will ever solve
                              (heh heh heh, heh heh heh...)

So yr bent in yr middle—
yr face is on the floor—
they take a great big club—
& beat you out the doo-oor
                              (watch it watch it

mr man
we're going to get you if we can

          that I'm alive today, I want to say, I want to say—
that I'm alive today
                              (heh heh heh, heh heh heh...)

I havent got a nickle—
I havent got a dime—
I havent got a cent—
I dont have that kind of time

            (all rite for you, friend
            that's the most
            we herewith
            propose a toast:

It's a hopeless world.

BLUES

Eighteen years I've spent in Manhattan.
The landlord was good, but he turned bad.
A scumbag, actually. Man, I hate him.
Money is green, but it flows like blood.

I guess I've got to move across the river.
New Jersey beckons with its sulphur glow.
Say, numbered years are a lesser evil.
Money is green, but it doesn't grow.

I'll take away my furniture, my old sofa.
But what should I do with my windows' view?
I feel like I've been married to it, or something.
Money is green, but it makes you blue.

A body on the whole knows where it's going.
I guess it's one's soul that makes one pray,
even though above it's just a Boeing.
Money is green, and I am gray.

NARCISSUS BLUES

Charity, come home,
begin.

W. S. MERWIN

When you rest your hands
on the table they rattle
like dice full of gamblers.
It's too long between feedings.
Then your wife is there, too,
begging for love, and while you explain
the soup gets dirty.
It's that damn gas heat
and she begins to snuffle
and calls you a toad
in a loud voice with the windows open.

It's as if you too could be
poor or insane
or need somebody
to hit, and your precise agonies
are nothing, and the brotherhood of pain
is spurious, and your tongue curls
like a harem slipper.
You're going to shave a stranger
backwards every morning
and not a word of thanks.

SPECIAL PAIN BLUES

Anybody can shout and holler,
It takes a special pain to sing the blues.
I say anybody can moan and holler,
But a special pain brings the blues.
It ain't about losing your last dollar
Or having holes in both your shoes.

Children cry when they lose they candy.
Babies cry when they wet theyselves.
Young folks cry anytime it's handy.
Blues comes up from deeper wells.

Takes a natural woman
To draw that muddy water up.
Takes a natural man
To cart that bucket home
And let you drink from the broken cup
And ease the thirst that's in your bone.
(Thirsty to the bone!)

Sometimes the blues so cold
It cracks the jar it's in.
Sometimes it's scalding hot
And burns right through the skin.

Stand it up beside Ma Rainey
If you want the test.
Anything less that folks try to sing
Ain't the real thing.

BLACKBOTTOM

When relatives came from out of town,
we would drive down to Blackbottom,
drive slowly down the congested main streets
    —Beubian and Hastings—
trapped in the mesh of Saturday night.
Freshly escaped, black middle class,
we snickered, and were proud;
the louder the streets, the prouder.
We laughed at the bright clothes of a prostitute,
a man sitting on a curb with a bottle in his hand.
We smelled barbecue cooking in dented washtubs, and
    our mouths watered.
As much as we wanted it we couldn't take the chance.

Rhythm and blues came from the windows, the throaty
    voice of a woman lost in the bass, in the drums, in
    the dirty down and out, the grind.
"I love to see a funeral, then I know it ain't mine."
We rolled our windows down so that the waves rolled
    over us like blood.
We hoped to pass invisibly, knowing on Monday we
    would return safely to our jobs, the post office and
    classroom.
We wanted our sufferings to be offered up as tender meat,
and our triumphs to be belted out in raucous song.

We had lost our voice in the suburbs, in Conant
    Gardens, where each brick house delineated
    a fence of silence;
we had lost the right to sing in the street and damn
    creation.

We returned to wash our hands of them,
to smell them
whose very existence
tore us down to the human.

HOW TO LISTEN

I am going to cock my head tonight like a dog
in front of McGlinchy's Tavern on Locust;
I am going to stand beside the man who works all day combing
his thatch of gray hair corkscrewed in every direction.
I am going to pay attention to our lives
unraveling between the forks of his fine-tooth comb.
For once, we won't talk about the end of the world
or Vietnam or his exquisite paper shoes.
For once, I am going to ignore the profanity and
the dancing and the jukebox so I can hear his head crackle
beneath the sky's stretch of faint stars.

WANDA'S BLUES
Ortega Public School, 1932

Wanda's daddy was a railroadman, she was his
    little wife.
Ernest's sister had a baby, she was nobody's wife.
Wanda was the name and wandering, wandering was
    their way of life.

Ernest's sister was thirteen, too old for school anyway.
When Ernest couldn't pass third grade, they kept him
    there anyway,
hunched up tight in a littler kid's desk with his hair
    sticking out like hay.

But Wanda was small and clean as a cat, she gave
    nothing away.

At school the plate lunch cost ten cents, milk was a
    nickel more.
Shrimps were selling for a nickel a pound—those
    shrimpers' kids were real poor,
they lived in an abandoned army camp, the bus dropped
    them off at the door.

Gossip in the schoolyard had it that Wanda swept and
    sewed
and cooked the supper for her daddy when he wasn't on
    the road.
She never told where she ate or she slept, how she did
    her lessons, if she had an ol' lamp...
That wasn't the traveling man's code.

Wanda was smart and watchful, we let her into our
    games.
Wanda always caught on quick whether it was long
    division or games.
She never gave a thing away except for her lingering
    name.

I would say it over: *Wanda   Wanda*

April, and school closed early. We never saw her again.
Her daddy loved an empty freight, he must have lit out
    again.
Wanda-a-a-a the steam whistle hollered. O my American
    refrain!

From AUBADES
epic exits and other twelve bar riffs

early in the morning
   hear the rooster crow
early in the morning
   hear the rooster crow
hear the freight train coming
   whistle moaning low

old grandpa stole away
   north by freedom train
old grandpa snagged
   that underground freedom train
booked his passage through the grapevine
   stashed his pack
and prayed for rain, I mean heavy rain

once was the north star
    then it was the L and N
used to be the north star
    then it was the L and N
not talking about cincinnati
not telling nobody where or when

going down to the railroad
    down to the railroad track
going down to the railroad
    down to the railroad track
grab me an arm full of freight train
    and ain't never ever coming back

AT THE STATION

The blue light was my blues,
and the red light was my mind.
ROBERT JOHNSON

The man, turning, moves away
from the platform. Growing smaller,
he does not say

Come back. She won't. Each
glowing light dims
the farther it moves from reach,

the train pulling clean
out of the station. The woman sits
facing where she's been.

She's chosen her place with care—
each window another eye, another
way of seeing what's back there:

heavy blossoms in afternoon rain
spilling scent and glistening sex.
Everything dripping green.

Blue shade, leaves swollen like desire.
A man motioning *nothing*.
No words. His mind on fire.

NOSFERATU BLUES

To be honest, I loved your awkwardness most.
Not the naughty plumage of your lips

Or the splayed wildcat of your accent
Or the unexploded heartbeat of your paintings,

But your uneasiness in crowds—
How you skirted the edges

And wandered companionless,
Fidgeted and tried to mingle.

What should I tell the torch-bearing mob?
That I longed for you like a lost dog,

Spent an undead winter wondering
What your throat would taste of?

How you sashayed across white-haired sidewalks
Into the end credits of back-projected afternoons?

Or just how your car flashed silver in the sun,
Your voice shot through with radio and slang?

Shit, damn, what does it matter.
I'd settle for some broken piano chords,

For a half-finished B-movie from the 60s
To walk around in.

Then again, you know, I know, forgive me, but
What South Carolina do you dream of in whoever's
      bed tonight?

What flaming hotels, what French aviators,
What ginger ale?

BED MUSIC

Our love was new,
But your bedsprings were old.
In the flat below,
They stopped eating
With forks in the air.

They made the old sourpuss
Climb the stairs
And squint through the keyhole,
While we went right ahead
Making the springs toot,

Playing "Low Down on the Bayou,"
Playing "Big Leg Mama,"
Playing "Shake It Baby"
And "Carolina Shout."

That was the limit!
They called the fire brigade.
They called the Law.
They could've brought some hooch,
We told the cops.

DOMESTIC BLISS

If I am as cute as a button
why have you spent the past hour
hunting for the one that rolled down your sleeve

onto the aluminum siding bus
carrying rows of disillusioned tourists
toward the chimney heart of our once famous city

Didn't you say that you didn't like that coat
that the buttons were too big for someone
possessing your delicate bone structure

Why isn't there more meat on this chicken
It's as if the damned thing began starving itself
once it knew what the future had in store for it

Is this what they mean by "organic"
I agree. We don't need to go on
fighting like this. We could learn

another way to fight, one that wouldn't
expend so many baccalaureates of bituminous energy
Perhaps a nap from which we would wake up

refreshed as fish dropped back into a forest pond
Okay, platinum mousetrap of a higher celestial order
one of us would whisper to the other

you get on your side of the rubber volcano
and I'll get on mine. But before you do
would you mind mending my hind paws

I need to get that sand back into my open veins

BLUES FOR HAL WATERS

My head, my secret cranial guitar, strung with myths
    plucked from
Yesterday's straits, it's buried in robes of echoes, my eyes,
    breezeless bags, lacquered to present a glint . . .
My marble lips, entrance to that cave, where visions
    renounce renunciation,
Eternity has wet sidewalks, angels are busted for drunk
    flying.
I only want privacy to create an illusion of me blotted out.
His high hopes were placed in his coffin. Long paddles
    of esteem for his symbol canoe.
If I move to the stars, forward my mail c/o God, Heaven,
    Lower East Side.
Too late for skindiving and other modern philosophies,
    put my ego in storage.
The moon is too near my family, and the craters are cold
    in winter,
Let's move to the sun, hot water, radiant heating,
    special colors,
Knife-handle convenience, adjacent to God, community
    melting free.
Eskimos have frozen secrets in their noses and have
    chopped down the North Pole.
The Last Buffalo will be torpedoed by an atomic
    submarine, firing hydrogen tiepins.

God is my favorite dictator, even though he refuses to
hold free elections.

I worry about the padlock I painted on.

My hair is overrun with crabgrass, parts of my
anatomy are still unexplored.

No more harp sessions for me; I am going to hell and
hear some good jazz.

Do you hear the good news, Terry and the Pirates are
not really real.

If you value the comfort of your fellow worshippers,
don't die in church.

Why ruin our eyes with TV, let's design freeways after
dinner tonight.

He might have lost some friends, but Jesus could have
made a fortune on that water to wine formula.

History is the only diary God keeps, and somebody
threw it on the bonfire.

The day of the Big Game at Hiroshima. The moon is a
double agent.

This year the animals are holding their first
"Be kind to people" week.

The Siamese cats will not participate and will hold
their own convention in Egypt. The civilized
world fears they may attempt to put Pharaoh
back in place on the throne.

For God's sake, Hal, jam the radio. Trip them with
your guitar.

HEAVY WATER BLUES

The radio is teaching my goldfish Jujutsu
I am in love with a skindiver who sleeps underwater,
My neighbors are drunken linguists, & I speak butterfly,
Consolidated Edison is threatening to cut off my brain,
The postman keeps putting sex in my mailbox,
My mirror died, & can't tell if i still reflect,
I put my eyes on a diet, my tears are gaining too much
      weight.

I crossed the desert in a taxicab
only to be locked in a pyramid
With the face of a dog
on my breath

I went to a masquerade
Disguised as myself
Not one of my friends
Recognized

I dreamed I went to John Mitchell's poetry party
in my maidenform brain

Put the silver in the barbecue pit
The Chinese are attacking with nuclear
Restaurants

The radio is teaching my goldfish Ju Jutsu
My old lady has taken up skin diving & sleeps underwater
I am hanging out with a drunken linguist, who can speak
    butterfly
And represents the caterpillar industry down in
    Washington D.C.

*   *   *

I never understand other people's desires or hopes,
until they coincide with my own, then we clash.
I have definite proof that the culture of the caveman,
disappeared due to his inability to produce one magazine,
that could be delivered by a kid on a bicycle.

When reading all those thick books on the life of god,
it should be noted that they were all written by men.

It is perfectly all right to cast the first stone,
if you have some more in your pocket.

Television, america's ultimate relief, from the indian
    disturbance.

I hope that when machines finally take over,
they won't build men that break down,
as soon as they're paid for.

i shall refuse to go to the moon,
unless i'm inoculated, against
the dangers of indiscriminate love.

After riding across the desert in a taxicab,
he discovered himself locked in a pyramid
with the face of a dog on his breath.

The search for the end of the circle,
constant occupation of squares.

Why don't they stop throwing symbols,
the air is cluttered enough with echoes.

Just when i cleaned the manger for the wisemen,
the shrews from across the street showed up.

The voice of the radio shouted, get up
do something to someone, but me & my son
laughed in our furnished room.

HEAVY DAUGHTER BLUES
For Yusef Komunyakaa

the t.v. is teaching my children hibakusha
i am in love with a dopefiend who sleeps under freeways
my neighbors are refugees from S.A.
and i speak negrese

the source is promising to terminate my train
of thought. the postman has put a hex on my P.O. Box
when my mirror cries do my pupils dilate?
i put my dial on quiet, my ears are gaining too much hate

> *i went to the clown show*
> *disguised as you*
> *you did not*
> *recognize me*

i dream i dream i dream
pass the pipe—please

put the gold in the shredder
Vietnam has taken Hollywood in helicopter blades
& kliegs
(let's arrest the runts)

i always withstand other people's hopes & desires
until they doublecross me. then we clash

i have proof that the culture of the biz-zi-ness man
is disappearing due to his inability to produce
one perfect realm of solitude into which
sanity can be delivered

when reading all those thick tomes written on God
it should be noted God is caucasian

the first stone shall be the last

the voice of our millennium is a niggah junky
gagging on stage
to heart-felt bass & trombone
pissing rhythmically in his jock
snot running into his forbidden funky os

now that machines have finally taken over
we can get into something serious
like art

> *i have my one-way ticket*
> *to the moon*
> *i am inculcated with the dangers*
> *of incriminating love*

after riding the desert in her '63 cherry cad
she uncovered herself beneath the sphinx
rut on her breath

the t.v. is preaching my children hibakusha
i am in love with a fuck freak who
lives in my alley

the constant preoccupation of a sphere
is in traversing the Möbius strip

i throw the symbols. i make reverberations

myth/my girlchild and me
cackle joyfully in the kitchen
as we make cookies
for the party of the world

THE THINGS-NO-ONE-KNOWS BLUES
After Wanda Coleman

I filed for bankruptcy in the borough of luxury.
I suspect it's time to eat my poetry.
My favorite turtleneck sweater, the green,
50% rayon, 5% cotton (rest unknown) one,

shrank in a tub of hot
bath water. A prisoner bit
a chunk out of my step-daddy's smile.
My mamma filled

her cancer with silicone
& pity. My wife dwells in
a house of critics. I'm younger than
sugar, but older than

NutraSweet because I had a birthday in
New Orleans.
I suffer various degrees
of wistfulness.

Honey,
I guess it's time I eat my poetry.
Cranked to ten my *Walkman* screams
static. I believe B.B. fingered

Lucille like the back of a pretty woman's knee,
but no one seems to agree.
Need pecks at the latch
of my *Wal-Mart* wristwatch.

The lines on my palms slope like portable ex
& why graphs. Baby, I suffer various degrees of
  wistfulness.
I suspect my penis will
be fed to a swimming Gila

monster. Occasionally Death
calls me collect.

THE ENCYCLOPEDIA OF RHYTHM AND BLUES

Passion killings, plane crashes, overdoses,
accidental and intended;

Suicides, bus wrecks, women;
the inability to choose between one

woman and another; heroin, booze, the inability
to choose between pleasure

and the Lord; men, prison, the white man,
the white man who owns

the record company; all of this delineated
as melismatic celebration

of disaster and the gut-wrenching agony
of joy, the anger and hush of the naked

soul alone, sighing and shouting intensely
hyperbolic declarations of erotic

heroism—*anywhere, baby, anyhow,*
skidding out of control and into the next-

to-the-last chorus and over the bridge and key
change, popping the balloon of a heart inflated

with humiliation and pain and replacing it
with guttural and shrieking glissandos

—*I once was lost and now am found*—
as if a singer were an angel commissioned

in the highest holy orders, as if a song had wings
extended into flight and feathers of shelter—

as if true love and its fraternal twin, the blues,
possessed equally the powers of devotion

and redemption, as if the one true heaven
were standing around the corner, laughing

drunk, and locked with lust and abandon
into the ever-loving arms of the mortal world.

FINALE

For Bessie Smith

My momma says I'm reckless,
　　my daddy says I'm wild
I ain't goodlooking but
　　I'm somebody's angel child.

BESSIE SMITH
Reckless Blues (1925)

BESSIE

    my Gloriana
My Bessie
Bessie Smith,
Enable me.
But first forgive.
Forgive my late arrival.
Forgive this late late rose.
Forgive the lazar place
That would not let you in.
Bessie, forgive my sin.
Forgive the chariot
That would not swing your way.
Forgive Mississippi, Bessie,
Forgive Mound Bayou, U.S.A.
Forgive.
And serve me,
Bessie, in this time
Of our most common need.

HOMAGE TO THE EMPRESS OF
THE BLUES

Because there was a man somewhere in a candystripe
    silk shirt,
gracile and dangerous as a jaguar and because a
    woman moaned
for him in sixty-watt gloom and mourned him
    Faithless Love
Twotiming Love Oh Love Oh Careless Aggravating
    Love,

    She came out on the stage in yards of pearls,
        emerging like
    a favorite scenic view, flashed her golden smile
        and sang.

Because gray laths began somewhere to show from
    underneath
torn hurdygurdy lithographs of dollfaced heaven;
and because there were those who feared alarming fists
    of snow
on the door and those who feared the riot-squad of
    statistics,

    She came out on the stage in ostrich feathers,
        beaded satin,
    and shone that smile on us and sang.

TWELVE BAR BESSIE

See that day, Lord, did you hear what happened then.
A nine o'clock shadow always chases the sun.
And in the thick heavy air came the Ku Klux Klan
To the tent where the Queen was about to sing
    her song.

They were going to pull the Blues Tent down.
Going to move the Queen out of the town.
Take her twelve bar beat and squash it into
    the ground.
She tried to get her Prop Boys together, and they
    got scared.

She tried to get the Prop Boys together, and they
    got scared.
She said Boys, Boys, get those men out of here.
But they ran away and left the Empress on her own.
She went up to the men who had masks over their head

With her hands on her hips she cursed and she
    hollered,
"I'll get the whole damn lot of you out of here now
If I have to. You are as good as dead.
You just pick up the sheets and run. Go on."

That's what she done. Her voice was cast-iron.
You should have seen them. You should have seen them.
Those masks made of sheets from somebody's bed.
Those masks flying over their heads. Flapping.

They was flapping like some strange bird migrating.
Some bird that smelt danger in the air, a blue song.
And flew. Fast. Out of the small mid western town.
To the sound of black hands clapping.

And the Empress saying, "And as for you" to the ones
who did nothing.

BLUES FOR BESSIE

*Bessie Smith, the greatest of the early blues singers, died
violently after an auto accident while on a theatrical tour of
the South in 1937. The newspapers reported that she bled
to death when the only hospital in the vicinity refused her
emergency medical attention because she was a Negro woman.*

Let de peoples know (unnh)
    what dey did in dat Southern Town
Let de peoples know
    what dey did in dat Southern Town
Well, dey lef' po' Bessie dyin'
    wid de blood (Lawd) a-streamin' down

Bessie lef' Chicago
    in a bran' new Cadillac;
    didn' take no suitcase
    but she wore her mournin' black (unnh)
Bessie, Bessie,
    she wore her mournin' black
She went ridin' down to Dixie (Lawd)
    an' dey shipped her body back

Lawd, wasn't it a turr'ble
    when dat rain come down
Yes, wasn't it a turr'ble
    when de rain come down

An' ol' Death caught po' Bessie
   down in 'at Jim Crow town

Well, de thunder rolled
   an' de lightnin' broke de sky
Lawd, de thunder rolled
   an' de lightnin' broke de sky
An' you could hear po' Bessie moanin',
   "Gret Gawd, please doan lemme die!"

She holler, "Lawd, please help me!",
   but He never heerd a word she say
Holler, "Please, *some*body help me!",
   but dey never heerd a word she say
Frien', when yo' luck run out in Dixie,
   well, it doan do no good to pray

Well, dey give po' Bessie
   to de undertaker man;
   ol' Death an' Jim Crow (Lawd)
   done de job, hand in han'
Well, Bessie, Bessie,
   she won't sing de blues no mo'
Cause dey let her go down bloody (Lawd)
   trav'lin' from door to do'

Bessie lef' Chicago
in a bran' new Cad'lac Eight
Yes, Bessie lef' Chicago
in a gret big Cad'lac Eight
But dey shipped po' Bessie back (Lawd)
on dat lonesome midnight freight

Lawd, let de peoples know
what dey did in dat Southern Town
Yes, let de peoples know
what dey did in dat Southern Town
Well, dey lef' po' Bessie dyin'
wid de blood (Lawd) a-streamin' down

MYRON O'HIGGINS

BESSIE SMITH

Oh, Tennessee road,
late at night—
where do you die
if your face ain't white?

MAE WEST CHATS IT UP WITH
BESSIE SMITH

You hadn't oughta kiss a girl if you're carrying a gun.
RAYMOND CHANDLER

once I found a cowboy   who thought he could
ride me into the New   West and God
put rollers on the bed   to make his journey smoother
last time I saw him   he looked the worse for wear
hair all but gone   gut eating his belt
he was a sight   all laid out in a new suit
(same one I bought him)

honey he had a corvette   and the morals
of a chinchilla   but just enough
gangster to satisfy my   Kansas City longings
oh he was handsome   as you know the devil was
in his eyes and his clothes   slick as sharkskin
some kinda silk worn close   and groin sweet
like morning rain   inside a buttercup

cept he dropped his pants and showed me
something for the cat to play with

thought he'd stopped me on the road
he did but when I said come up and see me

I was already heading in another direction
then there was that business   with some woman
he wouldn't name   now would naming matter sugah
you gotta know who you're aiming for   just aim
for the light   of one cigarette to the next
always someone there with a match   and an itch
to scratch   what hurts long as your voice holds

LAST AFFAIR:
BESSIE'S BLUES SONG

Disarticulated
arm torn out,
large veins cross
her shoulder intact,
her tourniquet
her blood in all-white big bands:

Can't you see
what love and heartache's done to me
I'm not the same as I used to be
this is my last affair

Mail truck or parked car
in the fast lane,
afloat at forty-three
on a Mississippi road,
Two-hundred-pound muscle on her ham bone,
'nother nigger dead 'fore noon.

Can't you see
what love and heartache's done to me
I'm not the same as I used to be
this is my last affair

Fifty-dollar record
cut the vein in her neck,
fool about her money
toll her black train wreck,
white press missed her fun'ral
in the same stacked deck:

Can't you see
what love and heartache's done to me
I'm not the same as I used to be
this is my last affair

Loved a little blackbird
heard she could sing,
Martha in her vineyard
pestle in her spring,
Bessie had a bad mouth
made my chimes ring:

Can't you see
what love and heartache's done to me
I'm not the same as I used to be
this is my last affair

LIST OF AUTHORS

Elizabeth Alexander b. 1962
Sherman Alexie b. 1966
Alvin Aubert b. 1930
W. H. Auden 1907–1973
Amiri Baraka (Leroi Jones) b. 1934
John Berryman 1914–1972
Maxwell Bodenheim 1892–1954
Catherine Bowman b. 1957
Joseph Brodsky 1940–1996
Gwendolyn Brooks 1917–2000
Sterling Brown 1901–1989
Darrell Burton 1960–2002
Marilyn Chin b. 1955
Wanda Coleman b. 1946
Billy Collins b. 1941
Jane Cooper b. 1924
Jayne Cortez b. 1936
Ida Cox 1896–1967
Robert Creeley b. 1926
Countee Cullen 1903–1946
Nancy Cunard 1896–1965
Waring Cuney 1906–1976
Toi Derricotte b. 1941
Owen Dodson 1914–1983
Alan Dugan b. 1923

Henry Dumas 1934–1968

Cornelius Eady b. 1954

Alfred Encarnacion b. 1958

Jeff Fallis b. 1977

Calvin Forbes b. 1945

Allen Ginsberg 1926–1997

Nikki Giovanni b. 1943

Nicolás Guillén 1902–1989

Forrest Hamer b. 1956

W. C. Handy 1873–1958

Michael S. Harper b. 1938

Robert Hayden 1913–1980

Terrance Hayes b. 1971

Sean Hill b. 1973

Son House 1902–1988

Langston Hughes 1902–1967

Major Jackson b. 1968

Honorée Fanonne Jeffers b. 1967

Blind Willie Johnson 1902–1949

Fenton Johnson 1888–1958

Robert Johnson 1911–1938

Gayl Jones b. 1949

Richard M. Jones b. 1925

June Jordan 1936–2002

Bob Kaufman 1925–1986

Jackie Kay b. 1961

Etheridge Knight 1931–1991

Yusef Komunyakaa b. 1937
Leadbelly 1889–1949
William Matthews b. 1942–1997
Colleen J. McElroy b. 1935
Thomas McGrath 1916–1990
Vincent McHugh 1904–1983
Claude McKay 1889–1948
Sandra McPherson b. 1943
James C. Morris b. 1920
Tracie Morris b. *c.* 1968
Albert Murray b. 1916
Myron O'Higgins b. 1918
Kenneth Patchen 1911–1972
G. E. Patterson b. 1960
Raymond R. Patterson 1929–2001
Willie Perdomo b. 1967
Gustavo Pérez Firmat b. 1949
Carl Phillips b. 1959
Sterling Plumpp b. 1940
Ma Raincy 1886–1939
Kenneth Rexroth 1905–1982
David Rivard b. 1953
Muriel Rukeyser 1913–1980
Jimmy Rushing 1903–1972
Sonia Sanchez b. 1934
Leopold Senghor 1906–2001
Charles Simic b. 1938

Bessie Smith 1894–1937
Charles Edward Smith 1904–1970
Mamie Smith 1883–1946
Natasha Trethewey b. 1966
Big Mama Thornton 1926–1984
Melvin B. Tolson 1900?–1966
Quincy Troupe b. 1943
A. Van Jordan b. 1965
Derek Walcott b. 1930
Margaret Walker 1915–1998
Anthony Walton b. 1960
Muddy Waters 1915–1983
Afaa M. Weaver b. 1951
Sherley Anne Williams 1944–1999
David Wojahn b. 1953
Charles Wright b. 1935
Richard Wright 1908–1960
John Yau b. 1950
Al Young b. 1939
Kevin Young b. 1970

ACKNOWLEDGMENTS

I want here to publicly thank the resources and friends who helped this book along; there are far too many to name individually, but particular mention must be made of Indiana University and Harvard University's W. E. B. Du Bois Institute for Afro-American Research, both of which provided valuable time and resources. I'd also like to thank Eileen Cope for her vision, Cathy Bowman for early suggestions, and researcher Steve Davis for finding last-minute birth dates. Above all, special thanks to Kate and Addie who put up with the hundreds of teetering poetry volumes while I worked on this book, and gave me that thing the blues so often search for: a home.

KEVIN YOUNG

Thanks are due to the following copyright holders for their permission to reprint:

ELIZABETH ALEXANDER: "Letter: Blues" by Elizabeth Alexander, from *The Venus Hottentot* by Elizabeth Alexander, copyright © 1990 by Elizabeth Alexander. Reprinted by permission of the author. SHERMAN ALEXIE: "Reservation Blues" from *Reservation Blues*, copyright © 1995 by Sherman Alexie. Used by permission of Grove/Atlantic, Inc. ALVIN AUBERT: "Bessie" by Alvin Aubert, from *Against the Blues* by Alvin Aubert. Reprinted by permission of Broadside Press. W. H. AUDEN: "Funeral Blues" copyright © 1940 and renewed 1968 by W. H. Auden, from *Collected Poems* by W. H. Auden. Used in the US, Canada, P.I., Open Market, E.E.C., by permission of Random House, Inc. Used in the UK and Commonwealth excluding Canada by permission of Faber and Faber. "Blues" from *The English Auden* by W. H. Auden, reprinted by permission of Faber and Faber. AMIRI BARAKA: "Look For You Yesterday, Here You Come Today" and "There Must be a Lone Ranger" by Amiri Baraka from *Transbluesency* by Amiri Baraka. Reprinted by permission of Marsilio Publishers. JOHN BERRYMAN: "Dream Song #40" from *The Dream Songs* by John Berryman. Copyright © 1969 by John Berryman. Copyright renewed 1997 by Kate Donahue Berryman. Reprinted in the US and Canada by permission of Farrar, Straus and Giroux, LLC. Reprinted in the UK and Commonwealth excluding Canada by Faber and Faber. CATHERINE BOWMAN: "Hard-Luck Resume" by Catherine Bowman, copyright © by Catherine Bowman. Reprinted by permission of the author. GWENDOLYN BROOKS: "Queen of the Blues" by Gwendolyn Brooks, from *Blacks* by Gwendolyn Brooks, copyright © by Gwendolyn Brooks. Reprinted by consent of Brooks Permissions. JOSEPH BRODSKY: "Blues" from *So Forth* by Joseph Brodsky. Copyright © 1996 by The Estate of Joseph Brodsky. Reprinted in the US and Canada by permission of Farrar, Straus and Giroux, LLC. Reprinted in the UK and Commonwealth excluding Canada by Faber and Faber. STERLING A. BROWN: All lines from "Ma Rainey" from *The Collected Poems of Sterling A. Brown*, edited by Michael S. Harper. Copyright © 1932 by Harcourt Brace & Co. Copyright renewed 1960 by Sterling A. Brown. Reprinted by permission of HarperCollins Publishers Inc. "Choices" [p. 235] from *The Collected Poems of Sterling A. Brown*, edited by Michael S. Harper. Copyright © 1980 by Sterling A. Brown. Reprinted by permission of HarperCollins Publishers Inc. MARILYN CHIN: "Blue on Yellow" from *Rhapsody in Plain Yellow* by Marilyn Chin. Copyright © 2002 by Marilyn Chin. Used by permission of

W. W. Norton & Company, Inc. WANDA COLEMAN: "Heavy Daughter Blues" copyright © 1987 by Wanda Coleman. Reprinted from her collection of the same title by Black Sparrow Press (imprint of David Godine, Publisher, Inc.), with permission of the author. BILLY COLLINS: "The Blues" is from *The Art of Drowning* by Billy Collins, copyright © 1995. Reprinted by permission of the University of Pittsburgh Press. JANE COOPER: "Wanda's Blues" from *The Flashboat: Poems Collected and Reclaimed* by Jane Cooper. Copyright © 2000 by Jane Cooper. Used by permission of W. W. Norton & Company, Inc. ROBERT CREELEY: "Broken Back Blues" by Robert Creeley, from *Collected Poems of Robert Creeley, 1945–1975*. Copyright © 1983 The Regents of the University of California. Reprinted by permission of the University of California Press. COUNTEE CULLEN: "Colored Blues Singer". Reprinted by permission of GRM ASSOCIATES, INC., Agents for the Estate of Ida M. Cullen. From *On these I Stand* by Countee Cullen. Copyright © 1947 by Harper and Brothers; copyright renewed 1975 by Ida M. Cullen. TOI DERRICOTTE: "Blackbottom" from *Captivity* by Toi Derricotte, copyright © 1989. Reprinted by permission of the University of Pittsburgh Press. WILLIE DIXON: "Hoochie Coochie Man" written by Willie Dixon © 1957 (Renewed) Hoochie Coochie Music (BMI)/Administered by Bug. All rights reserved. Used by permission. OWEN DODSON: "Guitar" from *Powerful Long Ladder* by Owen Dodson. Copyright © 1943, renewed 1973 by Owen Dodson. Reprinted by permission of Farrar, Straus and Giroux, LLC. ALAN DUGAN: "Swing Shift Blues" from *Poems Seven* by Alan Dugan, copyright © by Alan Dugan. Reprinted by permission of Seven Stories Press. CORNELIUS EADY: Reprinted from *The Autobiography of a Jukebox*: "I'm a Fool to Love You," by permission of Carnegie

249

Mellon University Press © 1997 by Cornelius Eady. Reprinted from *The Gathering of My Name*: "Muddy Waters & The Chicago Blues" and "Leadbelly" by permission of Carnegie Mellon University Press © 1991 by Cornelius Eady. JEFF FALLIS: "Nosferatu Blues" by Jeff Fallis, copyright © by Jeff Fallis. Reprinted by permission of the author. CALVIN FORBES: "Soledad" and "Some Pieces" both by Calvin Forbes, from *Blue Monday* by Calvin Forbes, copyright © by Calvin Forbes. Reprinted by permission of the author. ALLEN GINSBURG: "Sickness Blues" from *Collected Poems 1947–1980* by Allen Ginsberg. Copyright © 1984 by Allen Ginsberg. Reprinted in the US by permission of HarperCollins Publishers Inc. "Sickness Blues" from *Allen Ginsberg: Selected Poems 1947–1995* (Penguin Books, 1997) copyright © Allen Ginsberg, 1996. Reprinted in the UK by permission of Penguin Books Ltd. NIKKI GIOVANNI: "Master Charge Blues" from *The Selected Poems of Nikki Giovanni* by Nikki Giovanni. Compilation copyright © 1996 by Nikki Giovanni. Reprinted by permission of HarperCollins Publishers Inc. on behalf of William Morrow imprint. NICOLÁS GUILLÉN: "High Brown" by Nicolás Guillén, translated by Langston Hughes, from *The Collected Works of Langston Hughes*, Vol. 16. Used by permission of David Higham Associates Limited. FORREST HAMER: "Arrival" from *Middle Ear* (2000, Roundhouse/Heyday Books) by Forrest Hamer. Reprinted by permission of the author. MICHAEL S. HARPER: "Last Affair: Bessie's Blues Song" from *Songlines in Michaeltree: New and Collected Poems*. Copyright 2000 by Michael S. Harper. Used with permission of the poet and the University of Illinois Press. TERRANCE HAYES: "The Things-No-One-Knows Blues" from *Hip Logic* by Terrance Hayes, edited by Cornelius Eady, copyright © 2002 by Terrance Hayes. Used by permission of Penguin, a division of Penguin Group (USA) Inc. SEAN HILL: "Joe Chappel's Foot Log Bottom Blues 1952" by Sean Hill, copyright © by Sean Hill. Reprinted by permission of the author. SON HOUSE; "Death Letter Blues" written by Son House © 1995 SONDICK MUSIC (BMI) Administered by Bug. All rights reserved. Used by permission. LANGSTON HUGHES: "The Weary Blues", "Morning After", "Beale Street Love", "Song for a Dark Girl", "Midwinter Blues", "Too Blue", "Note on Commercial Theatre" by Langston Hughes, from *The Collected Poems of Langston Hughes* by Langston Hughes, copyright © 1994 by The Estate of Langston Hughes. Used in the US and Canada by permission of Alfred A. Knopf, a division of Random House, Inc. Used in the UK and Commonwealth by permission of David Higham Associates Limited. MAJOR JACKSON: "How to Listen" by Major Jackson, from *Leaving Saturn* by Major Jackson. Reprinted by permission of The University of Georgia Press. HONORÉE FANONNE JEFFERS: "Big Mama Thornton" from *The Gospel of Barbecue* by Honorée Fanonne Jeffers, copyright © by Honorée Fanonne Jeffers. Reprinted by permission of the author. J. C. JOHNSON: "Empty Bed Blues" lyrics by J. C. Johnson. Reprinted by permission of The Songwriters Guild of America on behalf of Record Music. ROBERT JOHNSON: "Kind Hearted Woman Blues", "Hellhound On My Trail", "Love in Vain Blues" by Robert Johnson, copyright © 1990 Lehsem II, LLC/Claud L. Johnson. Reprinted by permission of Music & Media International, Inc. RICHARD M. JONES: Lyrics from "Trouble in Mind" (Jones) © 1923. Used by permission of Univeral–MCA Music Publ A.D.O Universal Studios Inc. JUNE JORDON: "Uncle Bull-Boy" from SOULSCRIPT by June Jordon, copyright © 1970 by June Meyer Jordon. Used by permission of Doubleday, a division of Random House, Inc.

BOB KAUFMAN: "Heavy Water Blues" from *Cranial Guitar: Selected Poems*. Copyright © 1996 by Eileen Kaufmann. Reprinted with the permission of Coffee House Press, Minneapolis, Minnesota. "Blues for Hal Waters" by Robert Kaufman, from *The Ancient Rain: Poems 1956–1978*, copyright © 1981 by Bob Kaufman. Reprinted by permission of New Directions Publishing Corp. JACKIE KAY: "Twelve Bar Bessie" by Jackie Kay, from *Off Colour* by Jackie Kay, Bloodaxe Books, 1998. ETHERIDGE KNIGHT: "Feeling Fucked/Up" from *The Essential Etheridge Knight*, by Etheridge Knight, copyright © 1986. Reprinted by permission of the University of Pittsburgh Press. YUSEF KOMUNYAKAA: "Annabelle", "For You, Sweetheart, I'll Sell Plutonium Reactors" and "Woman I Got the Blues" by Yusef Komunyakaa from *Pleasure Dome* by Yusef Komunyakaa. Reprinted by permission of Wesleyan University Press. LEADBELLY: "Good Mornin' Blues": New Words & New Music Arranged by Huddie Ledbetter. Edited and New Additional Material by Alan Lomax. TRO © Copyright 1959 (Renewed) Folkways Music Publishers, Inc., New York, NY. Used by Permission. WILLIAM MATTHEWS: "Narcissus Blues" from *Selected Poems and Translations, 1969–1991* by William Matthews. Copyright © 1992 by William Matthews. Reprinted by permission of Houghton Mifflin Company. All rights reserved. THOMAS MCGRATH: "Gone Away Blues" from *Selected Poems 1938-1988*. Copyright © 1988 by Thomas McGrath. Reprinted with the permission of Copper Canyon Press, P.O. Box 271, Port Townsend, WA 98368-0271. SANDRA MCPHERSON: "Bad Mother Blues" from *The God of Indeterminacy: Poems*. Copyright 1992 by Sandra McPherson. Used with permission of the poet and the University of Illinois Press. TRACIE MORRIS: "Get Away 1928" from

252

Intermissions by Tracie Morris, copyright © 1998 by Tracie Morris. Used by permission of Soft Skull Press, Inc. ALBERT MURRAY: Excerpt from "Aubades" from *Conjugations and Reiterations* by Albert Murray, copyright © 2001 by Albert Murray. Used in US, Canada, P.I., Open Market, E.E.C., by permission of Pantheon Books, a division of Random House, Inc. Used in the UK by permission of The Wylie Agency (UK) Ltd. KENNETH PATCHEN: "Lonesome Boy Blues" by Kenneth Patchen, from *The Collected Poems of Kenneth Patchen*, copyright © 1952 by Kenneth Patchen. Reprinted by permission of New Directions Publishing Corp. G. E. PATTERSON: "Cinderella" copyright © 1999 by G. E. Patterson. Reprinted from *Tug* with permission of Graywolf Press, Saint Paul, Minnesota. WILLIE PERDOMO: "Song for Langston" from *Where a Nickel Costs a Dime* by Willie Perdomo. Copyright © 1996 by Willie Perdomo. Used by permission of W. W. Norton & Company, Inc. in the US and in the UK by permission of Marie Brown Associates. GUSTAVO PÉREZ-FIRMAT: "Bilingual Blues" by Gustavo Pérez-Firmat, from *Bilingual Blues* by Gustavo Pérez-Firmat. Copyright © 1995 by Gustavo Pérez-Firmat. Reprinted by permission of the Bilingual Press/Editorial Bilinge. CARL PHILLIPS: "Blue" by Carl Phillips, from *In The Blood* by Carl Phillips. Copyright © 1992 by Carl Phillips. Reprinted with the permission of Northeastern University Press. KENNETH REXROTH: "Married Blues" by Kenneth Rexroth, from *Collected Shorter Poems*, copyright © 1966, 1963, 1962, 1952, 1949, 1940 by Kenneth Rexroth. Reprinted by permission of New Directions Publishing Corp. MURIEL RUKEYSER: Reprinted by permission of International Creative Management, Inc. Copyright © by William Rukeyser. JAMES RUSHING: "Sent For You Yesterday". Words by James

Rushing. Music by Count Basie and Eddie Durham. © 1939 Bregman Vocco Conn Ltd., USA, Warner Chappell Music Ltd., London W6 8BS. Reproduced by permission of International Music Publications Ltd. All Rights Reserved. DAVID RIVARD: "Not Guilty" copyright © 2000 by David Rivard. Reprinted from *Bewitched Playground* with permission of Graywolf Press, Saint Paul, Minnesota. SONIA SANCHEZ: "Blues Haikus", pp. 39, 40, 60, 68, 69, 16, and 17, "Haiku", p. 61, by Sonia Sanchez, from *Like the Singing Coming off the Drums* by Sonia Sanchez. Copyright © 1998 by Sonia Sanchez. Reprinted by permission of Beacon Press, Boston. "Set No. 2" by Sonia Sanchez, from *Wounded in the House of a Friend* by Sonia Sanchez. Copyright © 1995 by Sonia Sanchez. Reprinted by permission of Beacon Press, Boston. "Blues" by Sonia Sanchez, from *I've Been A Woman* by Sonia Sanchez, copyright © 1978, 1985 by Sonia Sanchez, reprinted by permission of Third World Press, Inc., Chicago, Illinois. CHARLES SIMIC: "Bed Music" from *Walking The Black Cat*, copyright © 1996 by Charles Simic, reprinted by permission of Harcourt, Inc. BESSIE SMITH: "Backwater Blues" lyrics by Bessie Smith. Reprinted with permission of MPL Communications Limited. Lyrics from "Gimme a Pigfoot and a Bottle of Beer" (WILSON) © 1923 and "See-See Rider Blues" (WILLIAMS) © 1923 Used by permission of Univeral–Northern Music Co. MELVIN TOLSON: Reprinted from *Gallery of Harlem Portraits* by Melvin B. Tolson, by permission of the University of Missouri Press. Copyright © 1979 by the Curators of the University of Missouri. NATASHA TRETHEWEY: "At the Station" copyright © 2000 by Natasha Trethewey. Reprinted from *Domestic Work* with permission of Graywolf Press, Saint Paul, Minnesota. QUINCY TROUPE: "Woke Up Crying the Blues" from *Transcircularities: New and Selected Poems.* Copyright © 2002 by Quincy Troupe. Reprinted with the permission of Coffee House Press, Minneapolis, Minnesota. DEREK WALCOTT: "Blues" from *Collected Poems 1948–1984* by Derek Walcott. Copyright © 1986 by Derek Walcott. Reprinted in the US and Canada by permission of Farrar, Straus and Giroux, LLC. Reprinted in the UK and Commonwealth excluding Canada by permission of Faber and Faber. MARGARET WALKER: "Inflation Blues" by Margaret Walker, from *This Is My Century: New and Collected Poems* by Margaret Walker. Reprinted by permission of The University of Georgia Press. AFAA M. WEAVER: "Rambling (in Lewisburg Prison)" by Afaa M. Weaver. Copyright © by Afaa M. Weaver. Reprinted by permission of the author. SHIRLEY ANNE WILLIAMS: "Any Woman's Blues" by Shirley Anne Williams, from *The Peacock Poems* by Shirley Anne Williams. Reprinted by permission of Wesleyan University Press. DAVID WOJAHN: "John Berryman Listening to Robert Johnson's King of the Delta Blues, January 1972" from *Mystery Train* by David Wojahn, copyright © 1990. Reprinted by permission of the University of Pittsburgh Press. CHARLES WRIGHT: "Poem Almost Wholly in My Own Manner" from *Negative Blue* by Charles Wright. Copyright © 2000 by Charles Wright. Reprinted by permission of Farrar, Straus and Giroux, LLC. RICHARD WRIGHT: "Red Clay Blues" by Richard Wright and Langston Hughes and "The FB Eye Blues" by Richard Wright from *The Richard Wright Reader*, 1978. By permission of The Wright Estate. JOHN YAU: "Domestic Bliss" from *Borrowed Love Poems* by John Yau, copyright © 2002 by John Yau. Used by permission of Viking Penguin, a division of Penguin Group (USA) Inc. AL YOUNG: "The Blues Don't Change" by Al Young. Used with permission of the publisher. "The Blues Don't Change" from

Heaven: Collected Poems 1956-1990, published by Creative Arts Book Company, Berkeley, California, copyright © 1990. KEVIN YOUNG: "Langston Hughes" and excerpt from *To Repel Ghosts* by Kevin Young published by Zoland Books, an imprint of Steerforth Press of South Royalton, Vermont. Copyright © 2001 by Kevin Young.

Although every effort has been made to trace and contact copyright holders, in a few instances this has not been possible. If notified, the publishers will be pleased to rectify any omission in future editions.